Guidelines

VOL 30 / PART 2
May–August 2014

Commissioned by **David Spriggs;** *Edi*

Guidelines © BRF 2014

The Bible Reading Fellowship
15 The Chambers, Vineyard, Abingdon OX14 3FE
Tel: 01865 319700; Fax: 01865 319701
E-mail: enquiries@brf.org.uk; Website: www.brf.org.uk

ISBN 978 0 85746 037 0

Distributed in Australia by Mediacom Education Inc., PO Box 610, Unley, SA 5061.
Tel: 1800 811 311; Fax: 08 8297 8719;
E-mail: admin@mediacom.org.au
Available also from all good Christian bookshops in Australia.
For individual and group subscriptions in Australia:
Mrs Rosemary Morrall, PO Box W35, Wanniassa, ACT 2903.

Distributed in New Zealand by Scripture Union Wholesale, PO Box 760, Wellington
Tel: 04 385 0421; Fax: 04 384 3990; E-mail: suwholesale@clear.net.nz

Publications distributed to more than 60 countries

Acknowledgments
The New Revised Standard Version of the Bible, Anglicised edition, copyright © 1989, 1995 by the
Division of Christian Education of the National Council of the Churches of Christ in the USA.
Used by permission. All rights reserved.

The Holy Bible, New International Version, Anglicised edition, copyright © 1979, 1984, 2011 by
Biblica. Used by permission of Hodder & Stoughton Publishers, an Hachette UK company. All
rights reserved. 'NIV' is a registered trademark of Biblica. UK trademark number 1448790.

The Revised Standard Version of the Bible, copyright © 1946, 1952, 1971 by the Division of Christian Education of the National Council of the Churches of Christ in the USA. Used by permission.
All rights reserved.

Scripture quotations marked (ESV) are from The Holy Bible, English Standard Version, published
by HarperCollins Publishers © 2001 Crossway Bibles, a division of Good News Publishers. Used
by permission. All rights reserved.

The New American Standard Bible, copyright © 1960, 1962, 1963, 1968, 1971, 1972, 1973, 1975,
1977, 1995 by The Lockman Foundation. Used by permission.

Printed by Gutenberg Press, Tarxien, Malta.

Suggestions for using *Guidelines*

Set aside a regular time and place, if possible, when you can read and pray undisturbed. Before you begin, take time to be still and, if you find it helpful, use the BRF prayer.

In *Guidelines*, the introductory section provides context for the passages or themes to be studied, while the units of comment can be used daily, weekly, or whatever best fits your timetable. You will need a Bible (more than one if you want to compare different translations) as Bible passages are not included. At the end of each week is a 'Guidelines' section, offering further thoughts about, or practical application of what you have been studying.

Occasionally, you may read something in *Guidelines* that you find particularly challenging, even uncomfortable. This is inevitable in a series of notes which draws on a wide spectrum of contributors, and doesn't believe in ducking difficult issues. Indeed, we believe that *Guidelines* readers much prefer thought-provoking material to a bland diet that only confirms what they already think.

If you do disagree with a contributor, you may find it helpful to go through these three steps. First, think about why you feel uncomfortable. Perhaps this is an idea that is new to you, or you are not happy at the way something has been expressed. Or there may be something more substantial—you may feel that the writer is guilty of sweeping generalisation, factual error, theological or ethical misjudgment. Second, pray that God would use this disagreement to teach you more about his word and about yourself. Third, think about what you will do as a result of the disagreement. You might resolve to find out more about the issue, or write to the contributor or the editors of *Guidelines*.

To send feedback, you may email or write to BRF at the addresses shown opposite. If you would like your comment to be included on our website, please email connect@brf.org.uk. You can also Tweet to @brfonline, using the hashtag #brfconnect.

Writers in this issue

Andrew Lincoln is Emeritus Professor of New Testament at the University of Gloucestershire. His publications include substantial commentaries on Ephesians, Colossians and the Gospel of John.

Brian Howell is Tutor in Old Testament on the West of England Ministerial Training Course at Redcliffe College, Gloucester.

Jason Clark is a senior leader of Vineyard Church, Sutton. He is completing his PhD research on the church and consumer culture, and teaches regularly at church conferences and at seminaries in the UK, Europe and US.

Anne Richards is the convenor of the ecumenical Mission Theology Advisory Group and the National Adviser to the Archbishops' Council on mission theology, alternative spiritualities and new religious movements.

Tom Wilson is vicar of St James and Christ Church in the centre of Gloucester. He enjoys the challenge of urban ministry, but is saddened by the number of people he meets who have much to lament.

Hugh Williamson is Regius Professor of Hebrew at Oxford University. He has written extensively on Chronicles, Ezra, Nehemiah and Isaiah.

Joanne Cox is a Methodist presbyter in Westminster, and the Evangelism in Contemporary Culture officer for the Methodist Church. She is the chair of the Christian Enquiries Agency and a trustee of Share Jesus International.

Jeremy Duff is Team Vicar in South Widnes. His teaching and writing ministry has included posts at Liverpool Cathedral and Oxford University.

Nigel G. Wright was Principal of Spurgeon's College from 2000 to 2013 and is a former President of the Baptist Union of Great Britain.

Stuart Murray-Williams works under the auspices of the Anabaptist Network as a trainer and consultant, with particular interest in urban mission, church planting and emerging forms of church.

Simon Springett leaves the Royal Navy this year after over 20 years as a commando trained chaplain. His most recent deployment, to Afghanistan with the Royal Marines, included extensive involvement in supply convoys across contested areas of Helmand Province.

David Spriggs is a Baptist minister who has worked for the last 15 years with Bible Society, helping the churches and Higher Education to engage more fruitfully with the Bible.

The Editor writes...

World War I is very much in our minds as we move relentlessly towards the 100th anniversary of the day when Britian declared war on Germany: 4 August 1914. This 'war to end all wars' reminds us of the horror of such all-embracing and destructive human endeavour.

For many at the time, responding to Lord Kitchener's appeal was a matter of national pride and courage, but, for others, it meant disobedience to the Lordship of Christ. So we have included two different and thought-provoking perspectives on Christian attitudes to war by Simon Springett (a chaplain with the Royal Marines) and Stuart Murray-Williams (a member of an Anabaptist network).

Our readings from Lamentations, guided by Tom Wilson, remind us that the Old Testament is a valuable resource for sustaining faith in the light of brutality and suffering. The material from Matthew's Gospel, expounded by Nigel Wright, also includes deep challenges to our Christian commitment, with its call for Jesus to be the absolute priority in our lives.

This issue begins, however, by discovering some of the riches of the letter to the Colossians. Andrew Lincoln explores the profound significance of the supremacy of Christ and the ultimate purposes of God, as well as the need to be sustained by prayer and to live our lives faithfully. Later in the issue, Isaiah 40—48, like Colossians, calls us to view life from the divine perspective. We are grateful to Professor Hugh Williamson for illuminating the core message of this rich portion of the scriptures.

Isaiah 40—48 is full of God-given hope as it confronts the realities of life, and so is our contribution from Joanne Cox, who until recently led the Discipleship and Mission department for the Methodist Church. She stimulates our reflections on the importance of community in this year of *Hope Together*.

Pentecost was the time when the church's mission became operational, and Anne Richards brings us biblically based reflections on mission, which also relate to the issues of war, peace and reconciliation. Another new contributor, Jason Clark, shares with us his insights about how we can recentre ourselves on Jesus and so gain the strength to live for him.

We are delighted to welcome back Jeremy Duff as he explores the 'I am' sayings in John's Gospel. Brian Howell completes his work on Chronicles for us, and finally I explore some insights about praying from the Old Testament.

David Spriggs

The BRF Prayer

Almighty God,
you have taught us that your word is a lamp for our
feet and a light for our path. Help us, and all who
prayerfully read your word, to deepen our
fellowship with you and with each other through your love.
And in so doing may we come to know you more fully,
love you more truly, and follow more faithfully in
the steps of your son Jesus Christ, who lives and
reigns with you and the Holy Spirit,
one God for evermore. Amen.

Colossians

To read Colossians is to be confronted by a 'big picture' version of the Christian gospel. In its comprehensive message, the Christ with whom individual believers are in relation is also the cosmic Lord, the one who integrates the universal and the particular, heaven and earth, the other-worldly and the this-worldly, the church and society.

There is, however, little scholarly consensus about the setting from which this magnificent vision of the implications of the gospel emerged. Colossians is one of the 'disputed Paulines'. Some hold to actual authorship by the apostle Paul (perhaps with greater freedom given on this occasion to the named co-sender, Timothy), while others are persuaded, on the grounds of style and other factors, that the letter was written by a follower of Paul after his death and attributed to the apostle (following a similar convention in other ancient writings, including letters).

It seems clear that the immediate catalyst for the writing of this letter was a threat posed by a rival teaching to the Pauline gospel, but there is no consensus about the precise nature of this teaching. Some scholars hold that it was a purely Jewish teaching, others that it was purely Hellenistic, and others still that it involved a mix of Jewish, Hellenistic and Christian elements. While debates about such matters affect some details of interpretation, their resolution is not decisive for appreciating the significance of Colossians' overall authoritative message as part of the New Testament canon. Its writer wants the recipients to be filled with spiritual wisdom (1:9), and the ability to live wisely is rooted in and characterised by thankfulness for the undeserved favour of God revealed in the person and work of Christ. The notes that follow will highlight these recurrent themes.

Biblical quotations in these notes are from the New Revised Standard Version.

1 Affirmation in thanksgiving and prayer

Colossians 1:1–12

Like other letters of moral guidance produced by the various Greco-Roman philosophical schools, Colossians follows the general pattern of affirmation, correction of rival views and exhortations to wise living. Here, the affirmation takes the form of reporting a prayer of thanksgiving for the letter's recipients, which in verse 9 becomes a report on intercession for them. Like other thanksgiving sections of Pauline letters, this one signals ahead of time some of the writer's later concerns.

His thankful appreciation of their response to the gospel mentions faith, love and hope—a triad of virtues familiar from, for example, Romans 5:1–5 and 1 Corinthians 13:13. Here, however, hope is not a virtue but the content of salvation—that for which one hopes. The additional description, 'laid up for you in heaven' (v. 5), indicates that this hope is not merely a vague wish about the future but an assured present reality. It reflects a perspective, found in Jewish apocalyptic literature, whereby the salvation of the end-time is certain because it is already secured in heaven. In Colossians, the content of this hope is Christ himself, who is at present in heaven (see 1:27; 3:1). The assurance provided by such hope counters any insecurity induced by the rival teaching's insistence on further means, such as ascetic observances and visionary experiences, as necessary for attaining full salvation.

In the face of a teaching that has the appearance of wisdom (2:23), the writer's prayer for his addressees is that they 'may be filled with the knowledge of God's will in all spiritual wisdom and understanding' (v. 9). The letter's one reference to the Spirit in the previous verse means that 'spiritual' here is to be understood in relation to the divine Spirit and that the wisdom desired is not simply an innate capacity of the human spirit but is integral to believers' experience of what God has accomplished and provides in Christ. If 'lives worthy of the Lord' (v. 10) are to exhibit endurance and patience and be marked by joy and thankfulness in the midst of trials and distractions, they will also require divine resources of strength and not just stoic fortitude (vv. 11–12).

2 Christ: God's wisdom

Colossians 1:13–23

The thanksgiving that is to mark the lives of the letter's recipients has its grounds both in what God has accomplished (a rescue act, delivering believers from the dominion of darkness and transferring them to a new sphere of rule, with its liberation from guilt) and in the one through whom God has accomplished it—God's 'beloved Son' (vv. 13–14). This thanksgiving now takes up the praise of Christ from what many consider to be an early Christian hymn extolling the supreme role of Christ in the spheres of both creation and redemption (vv. 15–20).

He is praised as the divine agent, the sustaining power and the goal of creation and, when the cosmos had become alienated from its purpose, as the means and goal of its reconciliation. Facilitated by reflections about God's immanence in creation as personified Wisdom or the *Logos* in Hellenistic Jewish writings such as the Apocryphal Book of Wisdom and the work of the first-century philosopher Philo, this hymnic depiction now sees Jesus Christ as summing up all that God is, in interaction with the cosmos: 'in him all the fullness [of God] was pleased to dwell'. Our familiarity with the language of Christian worship should not prevent us from recognising the staggering nature of such a claim, about a near contemporary of the writer who had been ignominiously executed. As a consequence of the impact of the resurrection on his first followers, they had come to recognise that if, through being 'the firstborn from the dead', the Messiah was preeminent in everything (v. 18), then he must always have had such ultimacy.

To hold this belief in our context is to be convinced that, whatever the vastness or age of the cosmos, Christ is its pervasive energising principle and that this principle is not impersonal but bears a human face. It means that, despite chaotic and alienating forces at work, the pattern of Christ's death and resurrection—and not the survival of the fittest or an unending chain of violence—is what gives reality its distinctive character. Quite remarkably, the wisdom of Colossians holds together statements about Christ's universal significance with the particulars of a bleeding and suffocating death in humiliation on a cross (v. 20c). His cosmic rule is achieved through his becoming a victim; his peacemaking is accomplished through the absorption of violence.

3 Paul: sage and suffering servant

Colossians 1:24—2:5

The Paul of Colossians has a unique apostolic vocation as the mediator of the divine wisdom embodied in Christ. He is the wisdom teacher *par excellence*, not just for those in the churches in Colosse and Laodicea (see 2:1; 4:16), who have learned Pauline wisdom from Epaphras (1:7), but for all people—'warning everyone and teaching everyone in all wisdom' (1:28). His role has involved not simply dispensing wisdom from a sage's study but also enduring immense toil, struggle and suffering in the service of the church and humanity (1:24, 29; 2:1). In his passionate advocacy of the gospel, costly mentoring of converts and persecution (see the later references to the chains of his imprisonment in 4:3, 18), this wisdom teacher has also been a suffering servant.

The latter notion provides most help with the difficult language about 'completing what is lacking in Christ's afflictions' (1:24b). In the light of the previous emphasis on the sufficiency of Christ's reconciling work through his death, it is hard to imagine that such redemptive suffering was thought to be in need of supplementation. In the undisputed letters, however, Paul saw his vocation as reflecting that of Isaiah's suffering servant figure (see Galatians 1:15–16; Romans 15:20–21). So here, in an extension of Christ's role as servant, Paul's mission can be viewed as actively participating in the same pattern of suffering that Christ experienced. These 'afflictions of Christ' are lacking as long as the work of proclamation is incomplete. There can be rejoicing in such missionary, rather than redemptive, sufferings for the sake of his Gentile converts because they are part of the fulfilment of God's purposes through the worldwide proclamation of the gospel.

The content of Paul's teaching is described as a 'mystery'—a hidden aspect of God's purposes that has now been disclosed and can be summarised as Christ among the Gentiles (1:26–27). The goal of this teaching about the Christ, in whom are 'all the treasures of wisdom and knowledge' (2:3), is that everyone should become complete or mature in Christ. Such mature and fulfilled living is sustained through a firm relationship to Christ and resourced by the riches he supplies as the embodiment of God's wisdom (1:28; 2:2, 5).

4 Confronting a pseudo-wisdom

Colossians 2:6–23

The wisdom that Colossians commends is summed up in terms of appropriating the tradition about Christ as Lord that its readers have received. Wise living overflows with gratitude for what God has done in Christ on their behalf, including their incorporation into the fullness of life available in him (vv. 6–7, 9).

Living in this way should prevent the believers from being seduced by the attractions of a rival philosophy or wisdom teaching, now mentioned explicitly (v. 8). In offering correction, the writer concludes that its advocacy of such matters as fasting and observance of festivals (v. 16), self-abasement and severe treatment of the body (vv. 18, 23), worshipping angels and visionary experience (v. 18) may have 'the appearance of wisdom' but is of no value for a genuinely full life, since these practices serve only to fulfil the negative sphere of 'the flesh' (v. 23). What makes the rival teaching particularly insidious is its apparent combination of insistence on such practices with belief in Christ (see v. 19: 'not holding fast to the head').

The writer's negative judgment of the alternative wisdom is not because its practices, taken by themselves, are necessarily harmful but because they are linked to a false assessment of the role of what he calls 'the elemental spirits of the universe' (vv. 8, 20), which in all probability are to be identified with the spiritual rulers and authorities mentioned in verses 10 and 15 (see also 1:16, 20). The pseudo-wisdom taught that, because of the inferiority of human bodily life, the spiritual powers ruling the heavenly bodies and controlling the calendar needed to be placated by ascetic practices and could be invoked through special visions in order to ward off other evil powers and provide further knowledge. To follow this teaching, though, would be to fail to recognise the security and sufficiency of the Pauline gospel in which Christ's supremacy over cosmic powers was demonstrated in his death, which broke their hold and exposed them (vv. 10, 14–15). It would also be a failure to see that the believers' identification with Christ's death through faith and baptism has liberated them from the tyranny of these powers of the old order, and that the regulations being advocated should therefore have no hold over them (vv. 11–12, 20).

5 Heavenly-minded: holiness and community

Colossians 3:1–17

In exhorting readers to seek what is above (vv. 1–2) and put to death what is earthly (v. 5: in the original 'your members on the earth', that is, physical bodies), it appears that the writer is emphatically endorsing the rival teaching's preoccupations with accessing the invisible heavenly world and its powers and with a rigorous ascetic attitude to the body. In fact, he does see the Christian gospel speaking to such concerns, but from a very different perspective. Believers have been identified not only with Christ's death but also with his resurrection, through which he was exalted to his present position in heaven. This means that their interest in the realm above is centred on Christ, and that seeking and setting our mind on Christ's supremacy in this realm are not activities needed in addition to belief in Christ but are the outworkings of what God has already graciously provided through union with Christ. Similarly, the exhortation to put to death earthly members is followed not by a list of physical parts of the body but by two lists of five vices (vv. 5, 8). Again, these sins of the passions and of speech are to be dealt with not by human efforts, techniques or practices but by recalling the significance of one's baptism: we may then appropriate both the death to our old person as part of the old humanity under the present age and its powers, and the life of our new person, now identified with the new order of existence inaugurated by Christ (vv. 9b–11).

The list of five virtues to be appropriated (v. 12), followed by the emphasis on forgiveness, love and peace, indicates the ethical qualities essential for living as the corporate new person in a harmonious and unified community. As space is given in worship for the gospel about Christ to be a continuing and abundant resource in the shaping of communal existence, local believers themselves, and not just Paul and his co-workers, are expected to become wisdom teachers in applying this gospel to one another's lives (v. 16). What is again unmistakable, through its threefold emphasis in verses 15–17, is that the pervasive accompaniment and natural expression of worship in particular, and life under the Lordship of Christ in general, is thankfulness for what God has already done through Christ.

6 Wise living in the household and society

Colossians 3:18—4:18

Inevitably our attention is drawn in this section to the first extant Christian use of the so-called 'household code' that, later in the Christian tradition, had detrimental consequences for attitudes to women and slavery. In its own context, it takes up traditions about the management of the three sets of relationships in the household that can be found in Aristotle and his successors in the Greco-Roman world and in Josephus and Philo in Hellenistic Jewish writings. These traditions reflect the view that the household is a microcosm of society and that, therefore, any upsetting of the household's patriarchal and hierarchical order is a threat to the order of society.

In addressing outsiders' concerns about whether Pauline churches constituted such a threat, this version of the code broadly accepts the structures of household relationships that were axiomatic in its time, while bringing to bear on them the Lordship of Christ with its potential for ameliorating and transforming conditions within them. So, for example, all of the groups addressed are treated as moral agents in their own right and equally accountable to the church's one Lord: husbands are exhorted not to rule but to love their wives, and justice and fairness are required of masters. In this way, believers will practise 'fearing the Lord' (3:22), which, in the biblical tradition, is the beginning of wisdom (Proverbs 9:10), and will conduct themselves wisely in relation to outsiders (4:5). It is often forgotten, however, that integral to the wisdom tradition is that its practical aspects are continually revised in the light of new data and changed circumstances. Christian wisdom will be to continue to discern how the heart of the gospel message applies to contemporary conventional values about the family and social structures.

Prayer, motivated by the letter's dominant note of thanksgiving, which keeps believers awake to all the blessings of God mediated in Christ, is needed for wise living (4:2). Alert prayer also intercedes for those who proclaim the gospel (4:3–4) and encourages those whose ministries constitute the links in the chain consolidating the Pauline tradition among the churches (4:7–17).

Guidelines

There is no shortage in our time of those offering wisdom about how to lead our lives, cope with vicissitudes and find fulfilment. Colossians claims that the source of wisdom and genuine human flourishing is to be found in God's revelation in the death and resurrection of Christ. Since the wisdom encapsulated in Christ is cosmic in scope, believers have been given the essential clues about their place in the cosmos and in God's creative and reconciling purposes for it, but they also know that there will always be more of this inexhaustible wisdom to explore and that their own grasp on it will inevitably be partial and provisional. There is, however, for Colossians, no inadequacy about the gospel's central message. What God has done in Christ does not need to be supplemented before believers can find in it an assured hope of acceptance with God and of spiritual well-being.

The confrontation with the rival wisdom in Colossians provides a reminder that Christian spirituality is itself contested: judgments have to be made about whether some versions of it have become too greatly assimilated to aspects of culture that conflict with faithful appropriation of the gospel. There will be occasions when health warnings need to be issued about certain forms of Christian spirituality—for example, those that are preoccupied with the supernatural or with other spiritual agencies in a way that detracts from the centrality and sufficiency of Christ, those that disparage the bodily or the material as inferior or evil and obscure the fact that humanity's plight is ethical, or those that insist on particular practices or experiences before a person can be considered a complete Christian. As we have noted, the heavenly-mindedness of Colossians, with its focus on the exalted Christ as Lord and its emphasis on thanksgiving, affirms life in the local church, in the household and in society, motivating believers to pursue fairness and justice and enabling them to find grace in the ordinary.

There can be no mistaking that, for Colossians, spiritual wisdom is measured not simply by its claims or ideas but by the quality of life it produces. How far Christians exhibit the transformative wisdom they advocate remains a hugely significant factor in their witness and dialogue about spirituality and human flourishing.

2 Chronicles

2 Chronicles 1—9 traces the story of Solomon's reign, which is preoccupied with the building of the temple. Indeed, the themes of Solomon's wealth and wisdom are subservient to it. His wealth reflects God's blessings for his obedience and enhances the beauty of the temple, and his wisdom also points to his obedience.

Unlike 1 Chronicles, which seems to have been written with a different version of 2 Samuel at hand, 2 Chronicles seems to have had 1 and 2 Kings pretty much as we have them today. The Chronicler expands and slightly re-orders the section on Solomon, omitting tales of his forced labour, his many wives and the temples he built to his wives' foreign gods—but Solomon himself is not the point. The main focus of Solomon's work, and that of the Chronicler, is the temple.

In a much more economical and pointed style than is found in Kings, chapters 10—36 follow the Davidic dynasty through the reigns of the Judahite kings. Unlike 1 and 2 Kings, which conclude on the dour note of exile, 2 Chronicles resolves on the promising tone of restoration—the return under Cyrus' proclamation. As its readership is made up of those who have returned from exile, Chronicles lays the baton of the people of faith back into the reader's hands. That is, it points not to the undoing of the Israelite kingdom but to its glory—a glory often veiled by the sins of its kings and its people. Upon their return, the Chronicler challenges and inspires the remnant to rebuild, by illuminating the ideal set out by their predecessors. Whereas Kings seeks to prevent Israel's history from being repeated, Chronicles seeks to keep the unerring plan and revealed glory of God from being forgotten.

Unless otherwise indicated, quotations are taken from the New American Standard Bible.

1 A builder and a place

2 Chronicles 1

Solomon enters the scene already established, in contrast with the account at the beginning of 1 Kings, which includes squabbles with his brother Adonijah (chs. 1—2) and a political marriage to Pharaoh's daughter (ch. 3). Also unique is the statement that the Lord was 'with [Solomon] and exalted him greatly' (v. 1). The writer is not putting Solomon's life under the microscope, but leads with the king's authority established by virtue of God's presence and evidenced by his success.

When Solomon dedicates the commencement of the temple's construction, he takes a curious turn toward Gibeon to make sacrifices, despite the fact that the ark is specifically mentioned as being in Jerusalem. The tabernacle had originally gone to Gilgal and then to Shiloh (Psalm 78:60, 67–69), where it was separated from the ark when the Israelites lost a battle (1 Samuel 5). While the ark made a circuitous route through Philistia and Judah, finally resting in David's tent in Jerusalem, the priests continued their duties at the tabernacle (1 Kings 3:2–4), now moved to Gibeon, where King Saul had reigned. Why not go to the ark, which was the symbol of God's presence, the very footstool for his feet?

In going to Gibeon, Solomon ties together the traditions of Moses and his authority and the Spirit-empowered wisdom of the tabernacle's chief artisan, Bezalel, with the power and presence of the ark associated with his father's kingdom.

Solomon, not yet near the peak of his wealth, also displays an extravagance in worship. A thousand sacrifices, if each one took only a minute, would take nearly 17 hours, but these were whole burnt offerings. The process would have taken days, if not weeks, to complete.

God responds to Solomon that night, offering what appears to be a blank cheque—'Ask what I shall give you' (v. 7)—which becomes a test of Solomon's character. Solomon's prayer is edited from 1 Kings 3:1–15, omitting the confession 'I am only a little child; I do not know how to go out or come in.' This characterises Solomon in Chronicles as already a mature and competent leader, actually heightening the nature of his humility, which results in God's blessing.

However, at the end of the chapter, we find an enigma. Solomon's name comes from the Hebrew *shalom*, meaning 'peace'. Apparently, though, Solomon's wealth comes in part from his sale of chariots (v. 17). The man of 'peace' was a tenth-century BC arms dealer!

2 The construction of the temple

2 Chronicles 2:1—3:1; 3:15—4:6

Solomon builds both God and himself a 'house', but, as the palace is mentioned only twice more, the temple is clearly his *magnum opus*. By omitting the material in 1 Kings 4, the Chronicler casts this project as Solomon's first official act as king. The temple building is in three parts: the preparations (2:1–18), the description (3:1—5:1), and the dedication (5:2—7:11).

The account of the preparation (2:1–18) consists of a letter to King Huram (elsewhere Hiram) of Tyre, surrounded by two descriptions of Solomon's forced labour. The Chronicler insists that this was solely foreign labour (2:17–18; see also 1 Chronicles 22:2), in contrast with 1 Kings 5:13–18, which states that the labourers were taken from Israel.

Notably, the description of the temple here is about half as long as it is in 1 Kings 6 and 7. Why would the writer abbreviate it? Jacob Myers suggests that the temple's significance is not as a building but as the focal point of Israel's worship (*I and II Chronicles*, p. 16). This emphasis is also reflected in Solomon's letter to Huram: 'Who am I to build a house for him, except as a place to make offerings before him?' (2:6, NRSV).

The pillars Jachin (meaning 'He will establish') and Boaz (meaning 'quickness') are of unknown purpose. They may have been gateposts marking the entry to the temple as forbidden to all but the priests (Carol Meyers, *Anchor Bible Dictionary*, p. 598). Their names suggest that 'they may have been personified as guardians of the temple threshold (see Psalm 24:7–10)' (Tuell, *First and Second Chronicles*, p. 126).

The bronze sea is 'molten' (v. 2, NRSV)—that is, cast rather than hammered metal—though probably composed of several parts. It stands on the backs of twelve oxen, three facing each compass point, and probably representing the twelve tribes of Israel. The dimensions of the sea are the same here in 2 Chronicles 4:2–5 as in 1 Kings 7:23–26, but the volume is 1000 'baths' more. The difference may be due to different shapes being conceived (hemisphere or cylinder), or the Chronicler's penchant for exaggeration, or the different (Persian) standards of measure. As in Ancient Near Eastern temples, where water represented the primordial chaos over which the deity was triumphant and bulls were an image of fertility, Israel's bronze sea represented God's sovereignty over creation and the source of its fruitfulness.

3 The dedication of the temple

2 Chronicles 5:2–14

The temple's location is not accidental. It is connected both with Mount Moriah, where Abraham was commanded to sacrifice his promised son (Genesis 22:1–12), and with the threshing floor of Ornan the Jebusite, where the plague that fell on Israel due to David's faithless census was halted (1 Chronicles 21:7—22:1). This makes the temple the place where both the heart is tested and God's mercy extended.

Solomon, unlike his father David, made sure to bring up the ark according to the Torah, with consecrated Levites carrying it, but with similar festive celebrations to David's, including loads of sacrifices and procession and singing. As Thorkild Jacobsen observes, in Ancient Near Eastern temple installation rites, 'Only when the image of the god in procession had entered the temple and the deity had taken possession of it could the temple truly be said to be finished' (*The Harps that Once*, p. 427). As in other Ancient Near Eastern temples, the cherubim served as a huge heavenly throne—except that in Israel it remained empty. The imageless God was thought to have sat upon the wings, with the ark as his footstool.

Verse 9 includes an interesting detail about the ark. Its poles, which could just be seen from the room next to the inner sanctum, were said to 'be there till this day' (see also 1 Kings 8:8). Of course, in the Chronicler's day, there was no ark: it had been lost in the exile. The poles were a reminder of what the Israelites had had, which could not be replaced.

Like the establishment of the tabernacle by Moses (Exodus 40:34–38) and Ezekiel's vision of the future (Ezekiel 43:5), the completion of the temple is signified by the divine cloud (vv. 13–14). God honours Solomon and the temple he has built with a display of his presence. The Hebrew term for 'glory' also means 'weight' or *gravitas*, and it fills the temple.

The dedication happens during the feast of Booths (v. 3; Leviticus 23:34), which also happens to be when Ezra read the law (Nehemiah 8) and when the law was to be read every seven years. This connection between the law and worship shows that the latter is not meant to be empty ritual. Those who enter the gates are to have 'clean hands and pure hearts', says the psalmist (Psalm 24:4).

4 A house divided

2 Chronicles 10

The next section of 2 Chronicles discusses the reigns of Solomon's heirs. Unlike the author of 1 and 2 Kings, the Chronicler does not synchronise the dates of monarchs in both kingdoms but only follows the Davidic line in the southern kingdom, Judah. This, along with the absence of the northern prophets Elijah and Elisha, evinces a view of the people of God as those who received the promises of Abraham, the Mosaic Law and the dynasty of David, and worshipped at Solomon's temple. All others are considered apostate (see v. 19).

This divided kingdom begins with Solomon's son, Rehoboam. His life is divided into three periods, the first and last (chapters 10 and 12) being of rebellion and the middle one (chapter 11) of obedient success. (If you have the opportunity, read chapters 11—12 to get the full story.) The first rebellion arises when the members of the ten northern tribes follow the former supervisor of Solomon's labour, Jeroboam, in baulking at Rehoboam's harsh demands. This gives rise to an apparent contradiction in the text. In verse 15 (compare 11:4), the people's complaint is said to be a move of God, foretold by the prophet Ahijah. This refers to the prophecy in 1 Kings 11:26–40, which describes God's intended punishment of Solomon's faithlessness by giving part of his kingdom to his 'servant'. However, in 2 Chronicles 10:19, the people of the tribes that would become the northern kingdom are accused of being 'in rebellion' against David's anointed. So is the rebellion God's doing or that of Jeroboam and his associates?

One way of resolving the tension regarding the cause of the rift is to see it as initiated by God (as a result of Solomon's sin, according to Kings) but perpetuated by Jeroboam. 'The schism itself... is the divinely ordained consequence of Rehoboam's own arrogance and unwillingness to "listen to the people"... but once divided, the continued separation, and especially the alternative religious structures required by the separation, become themselves the sin of the [northern] Israelites' (Hooker, *First and Second Chronicles*, p. 170). The key is that the Chronicler shifts the focus from Solomon's sin to Rehoboam's foolishness, and from the initial cause to those who prevented a healing.

5 The charge of the Lord

2 Chronicles 13

Rehoboam's tumultuous reign ends with the two kingdoms still at war. Although he is prevented by God from pursuing the northern kingdom militarily, great hostility remains. This spills over into the reign of his son, Abijah, whose name literally means 'Yahweh is my father', well suiting his dedication to rightly honouring God. Notably, when the two forces begin to draw battle lines, Abijah appeals to the northerners not to fight against him, for reasons that reflect the Chronicler's purposes: Abijah claims that God is on Judah's side, so the northerners cannot win (v. 12).

This kind of claim has been co-opted by opposing sides throughout history, so, in and of itself, it is not convincing. However, as the two sides here claim to worship the same god, Abijah's arguments gain teeth. He points out that the northerners took advantage of Rehoboam's youth and 'irresolution' to bring about the schism (v. 7). This defence of Rehoboam acknowledges his earlier foolishness while shifting the blame for the continuing schism on to the northern faction. More bile is reserved for Jeroboam himself, who erected the golden calves and replaced the priests and Levites with anyone who signed up for service (vv. 8–9).

As Steven Tuell puts it, 'Abijah, who trusted in the Lord and preserved right worship in the right temple, was blessed. In Jerusalem, the right liturgy is performed by the right personnel in the right temple; therefore, Abijah can declare, "We keep the charge of the Lord our God, but you have abandoned him"' (*First and Second Chronicles*, p. 166).

One question brought to light by this conflict concerns the large number of troops mentioned. The 500,000 troops lost by Israel (v. 17) are about as many as all of the coalition forces that faced Saddam Hussein in 1991. However, factors such as Abijah's short reign and his rather negative portrayal as being similar to his father (in 1 Kings 15:1–8) make it unlikely that the Chronicler would have fabricated a story. As short lives are often seen as a judgment by God, the exaggeration of figures to exalt Abijah would have been awkward and highly unusual. On the other hand, some have postulated that the meaning of the word for 'a thousand' in Hebrew might be 'a military unit', rather than a literal thousand.

6 Reliances

2 Chronicles 14:1–12; 16:1–14

Asa is one of the most positively portrayed kings of Judah, and the Chronicler's account of his reign is much embellished in comparison with the parallel in 1 Kings 15:9–24. The reign is divided into two parts, one of faithfulness resulting in blessing and one of unfaithfulness resulting in curse. Each part is centred on a military campaign.

Although Asa develops a strong military (300,000 heavy Judean infantry and 280,000 Benjamite archers), he does not view his security as being founded on them: 'The land is still ours because we have sought the Lord our God; we have sought him, and he has given us peace on every side' (14:7, NRSV). Asa's trust is initially tested by the advance of a million-man Ethiopian army. He is not weak, but he is outnumbered nearly two to one.

His prayer is illuminating: 'O Lord, there is no difference for you between helping the mighty and the weak. Help us, O Lord our God, for we rely on you, and in your name we have come against this multitude' (v. 11, NRSV). While many commentators find in this a plea from a position of weakness, begging God to help Asa because Asa can't help himself, it could also be from a position of strength. Typically, an attacker needs at least a three-to-one ratio to defeat a defender. Asa may be saying, 'Although I have strengthened myself, I will not rely on my strength.'

As so often happens, however, a victory of faith is followed by a defeat in self-reliance. Later in his reign, when the (very much smaller!) northern kingdom begins encroaching on Asa's territory, he hires King Ben-Hadad of Syria to intervene against them (16:3). Rather than clever diplomacy, this shows a lack of reliance upon God, which causes Asa to miss the ultimate blessing that God had for him. According to the prophet Hanani, God would have given not only Israel into Asa's hands but also Syria, the kingdom he had appealed to for help (v. 7).

Asa's faithlessness also begets cruelty. He begins oppressing the Israelites, and even puts a prophet of the Lord in the stocks (v. 10). This results in Asa's feet becoming diseased, which brings about his eventual death. Even then, however, the honour bestowed upon him at his funeral (v. 14) demonstrates that the evil he did in the last six years of his reign did not completely erode the good he had done in the first 35.

Guidelines

Although Solomon is an enigma, fraught with conflicting values, the Chronicler paints an unusually bright picture of him. He has a secured reign, mature leadership from the start and no sign of immoral excess, and oversees the grand and luxuriant construction of the temple of the Most High God. All of this is designed not to put a saccharin spin on David's son but to draw out the values that the returned exiles can cling to and extol in rebuilding the kingdom. Solomon's lasting achievement is found in the temple, which defined Israel's worship for the next 400 years. Its opulence reflects the power and majesty of God, yet it is set in a place of testing and mercy. Solomon's humility also defines how one should approach such a project, and is confirmed both by the wisdom for which he is famed and the presence of God that is manifested. The continuing presence of God is the very reassurance that the exiles need.

In looking at the schism between the two kingdoms, we must ask ourselves two questions. Have we, like Rehoboam, allowed our position, authority, calling or rights to overshadow wise counsel? Although he was indeed entitled to the service of the Israelite tribes, the manner in which he went about dealing with them spoke more of his pride than his position. Are we more focused on the respect we feel we deserve or the respect that we elicit? Then, have we, like Jeroboam, allowed the offences of others to excuse our own sin? In what ways are we facilitating a defiance of God's will or an alternative to God's authorised leadership, due to its faults? Abijah's stand against the northern tribes causes us to reflect upon our own worship. Do we come to God on his own terms? Do we honour those put in spiritual authority over us?

Finally, with Asa, do we trust God both in weakness and in strength? Are we using diplomacy, networking and other human methods, though not inherently wrong, to the exclusion of seeking God's glory?

1 Dangerous alliances

2 Chronicles 18:1–3; 18:18—19:7; 20:1–12

In 2 Chronicles 17—20 we find a story of a truly godly king, with just one fly in the ointment: he makes poor choices of friends. Like David, however, he repents and, as part of that repentance, he addresses both the religious education and judicial standards in Judah.

Jehoshaphat starts well by removing the Asherim—symbols of the female Canaanite deity (17:6). However, he then decides to align himself with the northern kingdom through marriage and is 'enticed', along with King Ahab, into a prophetically condemned battle against Aram at Ramoth-gilead. 'Enticed' (18:19–21) is the same word that was used of Satan's action in getting David to order a faithless census (1 Chronicles 21:1). After nearly dying in battle as Ahab's 'ally', Jehoshaphat is rebuked by another prophet for helping the 'wicked' and loving those who hate the Lord (19:2). In Solomon's prayer (2 Chronicles 6:23) these groups are opposed to the righteous, and determined by their conformity to God's way of doing things. Wickedness is what eventually leads Israel into exile.

Having returned from this disaster, Jehoshaphat brings about some judicial reforms, adjuring the judges to execute their duties out of 'the fear of the Lord' (19:7), something that he himself has experienced quite recently. Jehoshaphat (which means 'The Lord has judged') also pleads for the Lord to judge the subsequent invading hordes (20:12). He bases his plea upon their common humanity: these nations, which are related to Israel, are the very ones that God forbade Israel to attack en route to the promised land (v. 10). Jehoshaphat lays God's own honour at stake, as this invasion is wholly undeserved.

William Johnstone notes how Jehoshaphat's response to the threat is an exemplar of Israel's conduct among the nations. He seeks the Lord and proclaims a fast (20:3)—only the second in Chronicles, the first being held after the death of King Saul (1 Chronicles 10:12). 'The present observance of humiliation before God by the submissive king *before* the encounter with the enemy contrasts directly with the lament for the death of the defiant king, who would not refer matters to God, *after* the disastrous defeat into which he has led his people.' Verse 29a repeats 2 Chronicles 17:10: 'What Jehoshaphat has been installed to do, he has done. Israel's vocation among the nations of the earth has been fulfilled in exemplary fashion' (*2 Chronicles 10—36*, pp. 95, 104).

2 Of priests and kings

2 Chronicles 24

Jehoshaphat's ill-fated alliance with Ahab continues to contaminate the Davidic line long after his death. Ultimately his bride takes over, killing the royal heirs and setting up Ba'al worship in the temple (22:10; see 24:7). An intervention is made by the high priest Jehoiada, who hides and then reinstates the last remaining heir, Joash (22:12; 23:3).

Jehoiada guides young Joash, who remains faithful during this time. One important example of Joash's faithfulness is the box that he provides so that the people can give their temple tax for the upkeep of the temple, now in a state of disrepair. In 2 Kings 12, the box is set up to prevent embezzlement by the priests, whereas here in 2 Chronicles it is provided because the Levites are slow to respond to the call for fund raising (v. 5). Notably, whenever the people are given a chance to respond in Chronicles, they do so with enthusiasm (v. 10). This would have been a challenge to those of the Chronicler's day who were looking to rebuild themselves; it poses a similar challenge to our day as well.

Upon the high priest's death, however, Joash turns. He listens to the evil advice of the Judahite officials, trading the temple for idols and thereby undermining his own life's work. When confronted by Jehoiada's son, also a priest, Joash has him stoned in the temple courts. The location is nearly as shocking as the act. It is a blatant defilement of the temple, as dead bodies, mourners and those who had blood on their hands were all considered unclean. Steven Tuell writes, 'When stoning is commanded in the law (ironically, this penalty is normally reserved for crimes against God, such as blasphemy or idolatry), the sentence is to be carried out outside of the town, where it will not bring defilement upon the community' (*First and Second Chronicles* p. 196) (see Leviticus 24:14). God's punishment comes in the form of an attack by Aram (Syria), the very country that Jehoshaphat, in alliance with Ahab, opposed.

Thus, after all the good that Joash had been led to do, he was buried in the city of David, but not among the tombs of the kings (v. 25). By contrast, his faithful mentor, Jehoiada, had been buried in the city of David 'among the kings'—despite being a priest (v. 16). Jehoiada is also said to have lived to the ripe old age of 130—another demonstration of the blessing of God on the faithful.

3 Punishment and perspective

2 Chronicles 28

Ahaz represents an unrepentant king who not only dives to new depths of depravity in worship but also gives up the kingdom's sovereignty without a fight. Ahaz makes his sons 'pass through the fire' to Molech (v. 3) in the valley of Gehenna, on the border between Judah and Benjamin—an area known for its illicit worship practices. Furthermore, he sets up altars around Jerusalem to other gods (vv. 24–25), strips the temple of precious metal to placate the Assyrians (v. 24) and adopts the Syrian model for an altar instead of David's divinely prescribed one (see 2 Kings 16:10–11).

In contrast with 2 Kings 16, this account of the pressure brought upon Ahaz by the Syrians and by the Israelite northern kingdom focuses less on their failed siege and more upon their destruction of greater Judah.

Interspersed here is a unique episode about the Ephraimites, returning home having plundered Judah, taking with them a large number of captive Judahites. They are met by the prophet Oded, who warns them of their sins and tells how this act will bring down God's wrath upon them. Several elders agree and so, instead, they use their plunder to care for the captives and return them to Judah. Although some authors see this as being a positive view of the north, it is more likely to be a back-handed condemnation of Ahaz and Judah. The Ephraimites (that is, the northern kingdom) never confess their sins of faithlessness, idol worship, rejection of the temple, and so on—the same offences of which Ahaz is accused in 'going after the sins of Israel' (v. 2)—and yet even they turn back from evil when confronted by a prophet.

After all of this, Ahaz turns not to God but to Assyria. Despite his large ransom, they come and lay siege to him, not his enemies. Although Jehoshaphat had to be reprimanded for his unhealthy alliances, he did eventually get out of them. Ahaz stubbornly remains in his and pays the price. His greatest sins, however, are in his effect upon the nation. He leads Judah astray by placing alternative worship sites in every city, prevents proper worship by closing the temple, and causes Judah to lose restraint in both moral and worship arenas (vv. 19, 25).

4 Reformation

2 Chronicles 29:1–19, 31–36; 30:13–27

Much of the material on Hezekiah (chs. 29—32) is unique to the Chronicler. He uses the framework in 2 Kings 18—20 but shifts the emphasis away from Hezekiah's struggles with Assyria and on to his religious reforms. Hezekiah is put on a par with David and Solomon (29:2; 30:26): as David was given the plans and Solomon implemented them, Hezekiah reinstates the temple after the apostasy of Ahaz.

The first step in this reform is to open the temple gates (29:3). As in Psalm 24 and in Ezekiel 40—42), this represents openness to God and his ways and purposes. It signifies God's presence and his accessibility. The next step is to reinstitute the Levitical order. The devastation and exile of the families (29:9) is seen as a result of the cessation of temple worship in Ahaz's day. Hezekiah's address is in language reminiscent of the Chronicler's own post-exilic day, when the order has again been reinstituted (v. 8; compare Jeremiah 29:18).

Notably, it is not just the temple that is rid of its idolatrous images and ritually cleansed: sacrifices are also made for the people. Two types of sacrifices are presented here (v. 31). The 'thanksgiving' offering, made in response to the blessings of God, involved giving a portion of the sacrificed animal to be consumed on the altar, a portion for the priests, and one for the worshipper, to be eaten at a sacral feast. The other sacrifice was the 'whole burnt offering', which was entirely consumed by fire (except for the skins, given to the priests) upon the altar. In this sacrifice, the worshipper was giving it all, with nothing material in return. It was offered for a variety of reasons, including forgiveness of sin, dedication of holy objects, a vow or a thanksgiving. Here the people are thankful for God's display of mercy. In fact, they overwhelm the priests with their freewill offerings, and the Levites are pressed into service to aid the priests (v. 34).

A final note on Hezekiah's reform includes his prayer for those who have celebrated Passover but not according to scripture. Rather than barring them, he prays for them (30:18–19), and his prayer is followed by God's response in healing them (v. 20). This makes a significant statement about the value of seeking God with one's heart rather than simply following ritual purity laws.

5 Hope springs

2 Chronicles 33

Manasseh's reign, at 55 years, was longer than that of any other Judean king, yet it became synonymous with idolatry. He reversed all of his father's reforms by worshipping the Canaanite deities Ba'al and Asherah as well as celestial bodies and Zodiac signs (the 'host of heaven', v. 3). The fact that the Chronicler refers to more than one Ba'al signifies multiple manifestations of the same deity, each named after the place where it was found (for example, Baal-Peor in Numbers 25:3). Manasseh was also involved in many occultic practices, all of which were expressly forbidden as sources of knowledge. This recalls King Saul's visit to the witch at Endor, and his punishment for this 'unfaithfulness' (see 1 Samuel 28:7–19).

In verse 4 and again in verses 7–8, Manasseh is accused of acting contrary to the word of the Lord. However, we are not told specifically what that word was; we are only given accounts of Jerusalem's election. God promises to remain with his people and leave his name on the temple only if they are 'careful to do all that I have commanded them, all the law, the statutes, and the ordinances given through Moses' (v. 8; 2 Kings 21:8, NRSV).

One question that is raised is how the author of 2 Kings can find nothing substantive to say about Manasseh, despite his long reign and impressive building projects. Rather, he finds Manasseh to be the final straw that caused Israel to be sent into exile (2 Kings 21:10–15). Even Josiah's subsequent righteousness can only delay the judgment. In 2 Chronicles, however, it is faithlessness on the part of the whole people of Judah that is to blame (36:14–17). This gives the Chronicler a wider berth in presenting Manasseh. The king's building projects are discussed, and, rather than being pinpointed as the sole cause of the kingdom's downfall, he ends up exemplifying grace. Manasseh is taken to Babylon (then still under Assyrian rule), and humbles himself, acknowledging his guilt (v. 13). Many of the same words are used as those we find in Solomon's prayer in 2 Chronicles 6, concerning the repentance of the nation: 'plea', 'hear/grant' and 'return'. Thus, Manasseh's fate in Chronicles serves as a harbinger for the nation as well as an extension of hope. Repentance is still possible, despite the distance that they may have strayed.

6 The year of jubilee

2 Chronicles 36

The organisation of the book changes here, from treating each king individually to treating the period following Josiah's reign through to the call for return from exile as one section. The section is structured using references to the prophet Jeremiah between the first and last exiled kings (35:25; 36:12) and in the call to return (36:22). Why might this be? One thought is that Jeremiah prophesied a 70-year exile (Jeremiah 25:11–12;

29:10). If 70 years are counted from the edict of Cyrus in 539BC, this takes us to the year when Josiah died (609). Each of the kings following Josiah was taken into exile, in Egypt or Babylon, so this period comprises a sort of staggered beginning to the exile.

This structure also lumps the final kings in with the exilic generation—that is, the one being called to return. 1 Chronicles 1:1—3:14 lists 49 generations from creation to Josiah, if Abraham is not counted twice. (He both ends and starts a genealogical section.) The exilic generation thus becomes the 50th, a significant number in biblical theology as it is the number of years until a Jubilee is proclaimed (Leviticus 25:10). In fact, the exile itself is described in these terms: the years of exile corresponded to the number of sabbath year rests that the land was due (2 Chronicles 36:21; see Leviticus 26:40, 43). This not only intertwines the fate of the people with the land but also shifts the emphasis. Whereas 2 Kings spends a good deal of time on the fall of Jerusalem (24:10—25:30), in 2 Chronicles 36 it is condensed to four verses (vv. 17–20). The emphasis is placed not on the fall but on the rising again (vv. 22–23; see Proverbs 24:16).

Just as we began with a confession from Huram of Tyre (2 Chronicles 2:12), here another pagan king, Cyrus, confesses the Lord as God of heaven and earth (v. 23). The statement is repeated at the beginning of Ezra (1:2–3) with some key alterations. First, the Chronicler says that the Lord is with his people so that they may 'go up', which puts the promises to David into effect with the people. Second, the goal of the 'going up' is not Jerusalem, to rebuild the temple; it is simply an honouring of God, the key to the Chronicler's message to the exiles.

Guidelines

The kings of Judah are evaluated by the Chronicler according to the extent to which they removed idols and high places and followed the Lord, yet the people are condemned for their own sins of idolatry. In what ways do our lives inspire others to worship the one true God? In what ways do we allow other philosophies and worldviews to influence our families, neighbours or churches, unchecked? Do we consider the influence of our personal lives on the faith of others?

With Jehoshaphat, we found that a faithful life can be marred by the alliances we make, which can have effects that reach down generations. With whom might we have aligned ourselves, as friends, fans, colleagues or intimates, in a way that compromises our allegiance and ability to follow God?

With Joash, we saw the importance of the mentors that guide us. Who has given spiritual guidance and protection to our lives? Have we internalised these qualities?

With Hezekiah, we observed the challenge of restoring God's order in the world and encouraging worship in others. This involves sacrifice on our part, both in elevating the place of worship in our lives and in consecrating ourselves to God. Rather than simply attending worship services, do we prepare ourselves to encounter a holy God together through thanksgiving and sacrifice during the week? How do we treat those who do not practise the piety that we do?

With Manasseh, we found that our actions sometimes have irreversible consequences, and yet, as long as we live, there remains the opportunity to repent. Perhaps even on a national scale, the Chronicler sought to hold out hope for repentance. If one as wicked as Manasseh could do it, cannot we?

Finally, as the Chronicler brought his history to a close, we saw him crafting it to demonstrate God's jubilee. Those who have lost it all and are enslaved can now taste freedom. There is a clean slate. Will we turn to the God who offers it, and live a life of worshipful honour and gratitude, as Israel was invited to do before the nations, thus fulfilling her calling?

FURTHER READING

Steven S. Tuell, *First and Second Chronicles* (Interpretation), John Knox Press, 2001.

Paul K. Hooker, *First and Second Chronicles* (Westminster Bible Companion), Westminster John Knox Press, 2001.

Carol Meyers, 'Jachin and Boaz', *Anchor Bible Dictionary Vol. 3*, Yale University Press, 1992.

M. Jacob Myers, *I and II Chronicles* (Anchor Bible Series) Doubleday, 1965.

William Johnstone, *2 Chronicles 10—36: Guilt and atonement* (1 & 2 Chronicles, Volume 2, Sheffield Academic Press, 1997.

Thorkild Jacobsen, *The Harps that Once... Sumerian Poetry in Translation*, Yale University Press, 1987.

Christ-centred living

The stresses and strains of life seem to multiply year on year. In our 21st-century world, surrounded by an increasing secularism, many of us struggle with fatigue, the pressure of comparing ourselves with others, a sense of isolation or disconnection, unfulfilled hopes, and the fear of loss. Perhaps, like me, you started this year with the best of intentions, hoping to develop your faith, to grow closer to God and gain a better understanding of your calling in him. Over halfway through the year, however, perhaps you are simply wondering where the time has gone.

For the next week, then, we will take the opportunity to pause and focus on some of these key challenges, exploring how the resources of our faith can be brought to bear on them. We shall consider how we might re-centre ourselves on Jesus, to find the power to live the Christian life we most desire and to face the missional challenges of our time.

Quotations are taken from the New International Version of the Bible.

26 May–1 June

1 A knowledge of grace

Ephesians 2:1–10

Psychologists know that although we are materially richer than previous generations, this does not make us *feel* richer. In fact, we most often compare ourselves unfavourably with those around us. Not many of us feel we have spare time, money and emotional capacity. So how, if we are all maxed out with our money, time and energy, can we ever get to pray, serve and give in the ways Jesus calls us to? The early church had so little compared with us today, yet they gave so much, so readily—even their own lives. How did they do it? In reply to that question, Ephesians 2:1–10 turns our attention to the most important things in life.

Verses 1–3 remind us that, left to our own devices, we will always use everything in life for ourselves. Sadly, that can apply even to our relationship with God. Perhaps we turn to him only in order to get the things we have set our hearts on, the things we think we deserve. Our primary problem, though, is that what we deserve is only the wrath of God (v. 3) —and we need to know that everything we receive from him is through grace (v. 5).

Being a Christian means an end to boasting (v. 9; see also 1 Corinthians 1:29). The word 'boasting' here means something soldiers used to do as they prepared to run into certain death. As in the movies *Gladiator* and *Braveheart*, soldiers would make declarations of what made their lives worth living, to spur them on to sacrifice themselves. So what do we 'boast' in? What do we declare to others that life is about, to help us through? Do even our prayers reveal the things we think we deserve from God, the things we are using to 'boast' our way through life?

Boasting is tiring! Instead, we need to move into the experience of richness in Christ (v. 7), and we do so by realising that we are already seated, today, at the side of the creator of the universe (v. 6). Any lack we may feel we have in life should be measured against the status we have now in Christ. Self-centredness means putting ourselves where God should be, but salvation comes from God putting himself where we deserve to be. When we understand that, our boasting becomes like Paul's—only in the cross of Christ (Galatians 6:14). Then Jesus becomes the measure of all of life, and becomes our life itself.

2 The hope of glory

Colossians 1:24–29

We all have a vision for life, a horizon we look for and move towards, whether it is the weekend, our next holiday or a longer-term goal such as graduation or retirement. We have hopes and dreams for the future, and we create our lives around the way we imagine the future to be developing. We shape our lives by making decisions about where to live, what work to do, and what relationships to build. Our life is made from investments in the things we hope for. Ultimately, as we look back, our lives will tell the story of our hopes and dreams and the investments we have made in them.

Sometimes, however, our hopes are not fulfilled. Instead, our story becomes one of fatigue, regrets, struggles and difficulties. Then, even with the advice of friends and family, the horizon we seek may become an escape from our challenges rather than the possibilities that Jesus can open up to us.

Today's passage shows us that, despite his struggles and difficulties, Paul succeeded in maintaining a hopeful story and vision for life. To him, what might have looked like needless suffering was, in fact, part of a bigger story, the story of the gospel. Paul could easily have wallowed in the struggles he faced, but instead he chose to see them in the light of what God was doing with him, through and in spite of those difficulties.

When we proclaim the story of Jesus with our own lives (v. 28), as Paul did, our story becomes that of Jesus. The result is that our lives become so full of the power of Christ that, like Paul, we will struggle to contend with the energy of Christ at work in us (v. 29). When that happens, we see life from the perspective of the best of it, not the worst. The work of Jesus—not the success or failure of our own dreams—becomes the measure of our lives. Who we are and can be in him becomes the horizon that we look towards—the hope of glory.

3 Living out the story

1 Corinthians 11:23–28

We do not live life in terms of theories, first forming better beliefs and then acting on them. Indeed, there is much that we say we believe that we do not act upon. Life is much deeper than just belief in our heads; it is a story that we imagine, rehearse and live out. When we come into work after the weekend, we do not tell people what we believed that weekend; we share what we did, said and experienced. Our deepest desires, longings and pains are retold with friends and family—or they are kept secret and held back from others. Therapists help people to articulate their story, asking questions so that people can share their feelings, experiences, decisions and understanding of their identity. This enables them first to examine themselves and then to explore, imagine and act out a new and better story.

It is helpful to understand our storytelling in the context of worship.

Worship means 'worthship': it concerns the things to which we ascribe worth. So what do our investments of time, energy and money reveal about what we worship? What do we say first when people ask about our weekends? What do we look forward to in the week ahead and tell others about? How do we choose the pictures and stories with which we document our lives through social media?

In the Lord's Supper, we retell the story of Jesus—not as a theoretical belief but as something we do (vv. 24–25), proclaim (v. 26) and experience. It allows us to examine ourselves (v. 28), to consider who we are and where we stand in relationship to the story. We are invited to make the life, death and resurrection of Jesus the centre of the content of our lives, and to share the deepest parts of who we are with other people, around the story of Jesus.

The Lord's Supper, or, indeed, the everyday meals we share with family and friends, can be a time to consider what is the centre of our story—the story we live out, not simply the beliefs in our heads. Are we investing our life in the death and resurrection of Jesus, or something else?

4 Keeping faith

Jeremiah 29:4–14

The Babylonians knew a thing or two about religious identity. Taking people captive, including the people of God, they gave those people two alternatives. They could either be forcibly subjugated and suffer terribly, or they could willingly assimilate and prosper. Assimilation—becoming like the Babylonians—meant access to the best jobs, homes and relationships. That path led to less suffering but also to a loss of identity as God's people.

The 28th British Social Attitudes survey (2011) revealed that of those brought up in the Christian religion, 40 per cent had lost their religious affiliation by the time of the survey. Even more sobering is the statistic that 94 per cent of people brought up with no religion had not turned to any religion in later life. Groups such as the Humanist Society, with the stated aim of wanting to see Christianity decline further, celebrate these developments.

How should we live in our mostly secular humanist society, where to be a Christian is to be in exile in a non-Christian environment? We might learn much from Jeremiah's message to the people of God who were in captivity to the Babylonians. The false prophet Hananiah had promised that God would soon take them out of Babylon (Jeremiah 28), but Jeremiah brings them a very different message from God. He tells them to settle down in exile, even to increase there, but to live differently, without assimilating.

How can God's people do that? By investing in the most important things in life (jobs, homes and relationships, vv. 5–6) but doing so with the welfare of the city in mind (v. 7)—in other words, the welfare of others. While most people invest selfishly in those aspects of life, God's people are called to engage in them for the good of others. That attitude made God's people fully involved in society, but not assimilated: it led to increase among God's people.

Instead of withdrawing from humanist society into our faith, or living just as everyone else does and seeing Christianity decline further, perhaps we can take Jeremiah's words to heart. What would it mean to invest in my work, home and relationships for the welfare of others? Perhaps it would lead to more Christians, not fewer, in our country.

5 Facing change

Philippians 2:1–11

In my church denomination and family, we have an axiom that we often remind each other of: faith is spelt RISK. We need to remind each other of that because, all too often, we fear the risks involved in exercising faith. In particular, when change occurs or when change is required, we dig our heels in, resist it and hope that it will simply pass by. Yet to be a Christian is to seek and embrace change. 2 Corinthians 3:18 reminds us that the process of change is integral to the Christian life: we are all 'being transformed into his image with ever-increasing glory'.

Often our fear of change is rooted in our fear of loss, especially of relationships and material security. Imagine that you were suddenly given everything you think you lack and wish you had. Now imagine, having received it all, that you gave it all away, for others.

Jesus did exactly that for us (vv. 6–8). Having everything—being part of the Godhead, in relationship with the Father and Spirit as the Lord of creation—he emptied himself and made himself nothing, all the way until his death on the cross. Our calling as Christians, the transformation that 2 Corinthians 3:18 speaks of, is to become more like Christ. Our calling is not to success or safety, but to risk all we are to become like him. In Luke 9:23, Jesus declares that anyone wanting to be his disciple has to take up their cross—in other words, to enter into loss, letting go of all that we have, for him and his mission.

In verses 9–11, we see how the risk that Jesus took, in emptying and humbling himself, led to his resurrection and exaltation, and Paul reminds us, in Ephesians 2:6, that we are raised with him, seated at his right hand. Paradoxically, the real risk that we face is that we may miss out on the experience of his resurrection power in our daily lives by *not* taking the risks of faith, picking up our cross and embracing the changes needed to follow him. If we can make that step of faith, imagine what his resurrection power might do in us.

6 The experience of community

Hebrews 10:19–25

One of our deepest needs is to be in relationship with others, to be loved and to belong, yet survey after survey in the Western world details how people are feeling more and more isolated. Our desire for community seems greater than our ability to engage in the experience of it.

For Christians, there is a new reality—an experience of the body of Jesus Christ—to be entered. Hebrew 10:19–25 invites us into this new relationship, where we experience a closeness to God (v. 22) and to each other (v. 25). Yet this experience of community can still seem elusive. Our previous encounters with church may have left us wondering if we have missed something.

Access to this experience is not automatic. The writer of Hebrews guides us through four key practices that establish us within the new and living way that God has made for us in the body of Christ. All of these four practices challenge us to engage with other people, rather than waiting for them to engage with us.

First, we need to 'consider' one another (v. 24). We need to take the time to reflect on the people around us and the ways in which we might help them to grow in Jesus. Have we placed ourselves in a body of believers where we are regularly asking ourselves how we might help others to grow?

Second, we need to 'spur' one another on (v. 24). This can mean confronting others sharply, even painfully, as it does when we spur on a horse. Do we allow others to spur us on, or are we too touchy to let people do so? Have we given permission for others to speak to us for our well-being?

Third, we need to encourage one another (v. 25), coming alongside to empathise and support. This support must accompany the spurring. To spur others on without encouragement and support doesn't work; nor does supporting others without speaking into their lives when they need spurring.

Finally we are to take action, with good deeds (v. 24). The considering, spurring and encouraging all enable Jesus to take shape in us, so that we may do the things he has prepared for us to do. In a world where people often expect others to do something for them, we engage like Christ and do his work for others. All these four practices are the gateway into the experience of relationship with him and his people.

Guidelines

When seaside rock is made, the letters are placed all the way through the sugar mixture, and then it is rolled and stretched. No matter how much pressure is applied or how long the rock is stretched, the letters remain legible all the way through it. When we come under pressure or when we are 'stretched' by life, can Jesus always be seen at the centre, present right the way through us?

Do we find that we are too busy to serve others? Or are we too fearful—withdrawn into our own relationships, job and home in an effort to protect them? Do we need to risk engaging with others rather than waiting for them to engage with us, for the good of the wider community?

Pray through these issues, asking for the resurrection power of Jesus to energise your relationship with God and your mission to others.

Mission: reconciliation and spirituality

In 1910, a famous conference on mission was held in Edinburgh. It brought people together to dare to think about the evangelisation of the whole world within the life and times of the people attending. With the great technological advances of the Industrial Revolution behind them and global travel within reach, a truly worldwide missionary movement seemed not only possible but also necessary and urgent.

However, that vision of mission was dealt a significant blow by another manifestation of human technological advance: the beginning of World War I and the devastation wrought by some of our most destructive inventions. The poet Wilfred Owen wrote that the 'rifles' rapid rattle' now replaced the prayers of human beings ('Anthem for Doomed Youth', 1917).

The reality of what war does to our hopes, plans and desires has brought a new perspective to bear on our understanding of mission: sharing the Christian faith with others cannot happen in a vacuum; the gospel needs reconciliation between individuals, neighbours, communities and nations. In the first week's readings, we will be looking at different aspects of this important relationship between mission and reconciliation against a background of remembering the events of World War I.

In the second week, we move to a focus on the bedrock of Christian spirituality that underpins our Christian faith and is still instrumental in making new Christian disciples. During World War I, the artist and writer David Jones witnessed a priest saying Mass and saw some of the hardest and toughest of his fellow soldiers kneeling reverently before the makeshift altar as the infernal noises of war broke overhead. Jones was deeply moved by the realisation that Christian spirituality—hope, faithfulness, awe, love for and trust in God—could persist in this environment and even overcome the horrors of the worst that human beings can do to each other. After the war, Jones became a committed Christian. The power of this first encounter with Christ in the Eucharist stayed with him for the rest of his life.

This story reminds us that the presence of steadfast Christian faith in the most repressive of regimes and through the most base and degrading of experiences offers hope to others who are struggling to make sense of a world that continues to be damaged and exploited by human beings. The witness of Christians in shared experience is important: the people we encounter may often be looking for the hope that is within us. What resources can we draw on to make us better sharers of faith and better witnesses to Christ?

Quotations are taken from the New International Version of the Bible.

1 Creation and fall

Genesis 1:28–31; 3:22–23

One of the important changes in missional thinking to have taken place in the last hundred years is that we have stopped assuming that mission is just something the church does and started to understand that mission begins with God. It is God's mission that we need to find in the world and to which we should add our own efforts. God's relationship with the creation provides us with the vision of what mission should be about, and God's action in sending Jesus to live and die among us and for us shows how God continues to love the world. If we really want to share our faith with others, then we have to offer a vision of a reconciled world. At the same time, we also have to try to understand why the world we encounter is so divided.

How do we know what God wants? A good place to start is with our readings from the creation stories in Genesis. The writer tells us that this is God's creation, which is known and loved by God and pronounced 'good'. The land and sea, the plants, animals, birds and insects are contained in a balanced and flourishing ecosystem in which the new humans can delight, be nourished and grow. They receive this lovely world as a gift from a loving God, but something goes wrong. Instead of working in harmony with God's mission, these new humans impose their own interests and desires on the creation. They eat the fruit that God has told them not to eat, and what they now know fractures the vision. This leaves them in a very different reality, in which they must struggle, with only the memory of peace and beauty to sustain them in a difficult and pain-ridden world.

World War I turned this picture of creation and fall into a stark reality. Millions of people lost the vision of a peaceful, plentiful world as men fought and died, leaving devastated families behind. The earth suffered too, as trees, woods and fields were smashed to pieces. The first chapters of Genesis bring home to us that God delights in the creation, so when we damage it in conflict we hurt God and break the loving relationship with the Creator. Mission requires repentance, rebuilding and renewal.

2 Change for the better

Jonah 3

Open any newspaper and the stories there will often make your heart break. So many terrible things happen, which we cannot predict and which we seem powerless to counteract, whether it's an earthquake or a school shooting. Mission requires us both to react to those who need our loving service and to be proactive in changing what is unjust in the world around us. Yet working to change the evils of the world can seem like a hopeless and impossible task.

We can sympathise, therefore, with Jonah. When God asked him to carry his word of judgment and his call to repentance to the evil city of Nineveh, Jonah thought it was all too much. He ran in the opposite direction. But God did not give up on him because his heart failed; God did not just find someone else to do the job. Instead, God kept faith with the frightened, angry, whining, overwhelmed person, so that in the end, as we find in this reading, Jonah carried out his mission and the whole city was saved. We may think that change like this is impossible, but with God all things are possible.

No matter how difficult we think it is to speak God's word in the world today—especially in a world that, even a hundred years after World War I, is still full of violence between groups, faiths and nations—a voice that speaks about the consequences of our actions, and what will happen if we do not change, can and does make a difference. Jonah's warning spreads out to the whole city when the king of Nineveh issues a proclamation: 'Let them give up their evil ways and their violence' (v. 8). There is visible repentance and evidence of change. Jonah's mission not only reconciles the people with one another but also reconciles them with God.

Our reading confirms for us that our efforts can bring about radical change and hope, even to the most evil situations. When the cause seems hopeless and too big for us, God goes on calling us to establish relationships, to rebuild but also to create something new.

3 Deliverance

Isaiah 61:1–4; 65:17–25

The people of Israel lived through terrible times of warfare and destruction. When they were defeated and taken into captivity by the Babylonians, many must have felt that their worst moment had come and that God had abandoned them. The voice we hear in these readings from the prophet Isaiah reframes Israel's relationship with God: God's mission comes with reconciliation. Isaiah 61 tells us that God wants all of his people who are suffering from oppression or captivity, or whose lives are blighted and broken, to be released, raised up and restored so that they can live their lives in freedom and peace. God also wants to see rebuilding and restoration of what has been broken and smashed by human enmity. This restoration, making beautiful what has been made ugly by conflict, is woven into the fabric of mission. We know that this is important to God's mission because Jesus began his own public ministry by quoting these powerful words (Luke 4:18–19).

If we look ahead to Isaiah 65, we find what Raymond Fung has called the Isaiah vision, or Isaiah 'agenda'. What is the purpose of mission? It is that human beings will be able to live their proper lifespans in peace. People who build houses will live in them and will enjoy the fruits of their labours. Greedy people will no longer use their power to overcome others and take away what they have worked for, so war will be at an end. God's promise is that, with human effort, reconciliation can take place and new birth and growth can replace conflict. Mission is not just about evangelism but also about social justice and about making people aware of what God wants for human communities. The final goal of mission is a deep and lasting peace.

4 Peace

Zechariah 8:12–13; Malachi 3:1–6

Some political philosophers (such as Thomas Hobbes and Immanuel Kant) have wondered whether war is the natural state of humankind—implying that peace is just the absence of conflict. We learn in the reading from Zechariah, however, that in God's eyes peace is not just a time of regrouping before the next war; it is a dynamic state in which human beings can thrive and grow closer to God. Working for peace and justice, then, creates an environment in which the gospel can be more clearly heard. Zechariah offers us a beautiful vision of human beings and the land enjoying peaceful fruitfulness, which is powerfully transformative. Something that was a curse can be changed into a blessing. Blessing, in the Hebrew scriptures, is related to the creative acts of God and the essential goodness of all creation, so it is important for a faithful people to be an active conduit for God's blessing in the lives of others.

Saving and blessing are important parts of the missiological vision—the belief that out of strife and human struggle a richness for all human beings can come. This looks forward to 'judgment', in which all injustice is exposed, healed and reconciled. God is on the side of the bereaved—those widows and orphans mourning a lost generation. The World War I poet Rupert Brooke wrote in 'Safety' of his longing for 'a peace unshaken by pain for ever', where 'war knows no power'. Zechariah imagines what that world would look like.

Malachi's vision speaks of God's desire to bring deliverance. All that is destructive in the world must be removed, as impurities are removed from gold and silver when they are refined, so that only what is good, beautiful and true is left. Yet we are not asked simply to sit back and wait for God to sort it all out. Being part of the mission of God means actively working to make this purification happen. It is our job to root out injustice and bring reconciliation to what has been damaged. When we do this, we demonstrate God's love for the world and create the conditions in which the word of God can be heard by everyone.

5 Transformation

Micah 4:1–8

Micah strengthens for us the link between mission and reconciliation. In order to become the kind of holy community that draws the rest of the world towards us, we must actively demonstrate a desire for peace and not 'train for war any more' (v. 3). It is not enough just to talk about it; we have to show that we are committed to peaceful and equitable living with one another. Christians can learn from this that mission and evangelism by themselves are not enough; there has to be visible evidence to those outside that we are the kind of community in which they can meet God and grow into a loving and fruitful relationship with and through Jesus. This is a challenge, as we can see in Paul's letters, which show his worries about the squabbling and power struggles going on in the early Christian communities (for example, 1 Corinthians 1:10–12; 3:1–4; 2 Corinthians 12:20–21). Micah's vision prompts a question: can new Christians find peaceful and loving homes in *our* churches, or are we too involved in our own vested interests and internal conflicts? It is surprising to see how many churches are not really at peace with themselves.

One hundred years after the start of World War I, the challenge to us is renewed. Today, the great powers increasingly involve themselves in conflicts in poorer nations. We learn about our own country's involvement in places like Afghanistan and Iraq through our TV screens, not through bombs falling on our own houses, so sometimes it is difficult to feel fully engaged or involved. But Micah's vision of peace and transformation makes clear that if we care about mission, we *must* be involved. It is our job to see that swords are made into ploughshares and that our governments take responsibility for restoration and aid in those countries where we have intervened. In order for our good news of Jesus Christ to be taken seriously, we must be seen to be involved in reconciliation, exposing the truth about war and injustice. Mission is about making and sustaining a world, through the creative and reconciling power of the Holy Spirit, where 'no one will make them afraid' (Micah 4:4).

6 Vision of a new world

Revelation 21:1–18

In 2010, one hundred years after the world missionary conference, people from all over the world came together again in Edinburgh to ask just what we had learned about mission in the intervening time. One of the important themes was our need as Christians to learn from our history and admit that we have got things wrong. Our past history in mission is not attractive, and we have to repent of those times when we from the West imposed our faith on people in other countries or failed to trust them to become missionaries themselves. People at the conference agreed that reconciliation therefore remains an important part of our missional learning.

Another important theme emerging from the Edinburgh 2010 conference was the importance of the 'mission imagination'. If we are to learn lessons, where do we then apply that learning? What does hope really look like? How can we share the incredible nature of the future that God wants for us?

Revelation 21 gives us a vivid picture of the end purpose of God's mission. It is a vision of an ultimate reconciliation between God and human beings, in which the creation is completely remade. There is no more death or suffering and no more grief for the dead. God comforts the faithful and evildoing is banished. This only means something to us, however, if we review our own history and become fully aware of the terrible things that human beings can do to each other. If, this year, we remember those who died in the trenches, we should not just think of this violence as 'the past'. God is demanding of us *now* that this should never happen again, because God's mission is reconciliation and new creation. We should remember that the Christians for whom this material in Revelation was written were experiencing terrible persecution. Just as World War I soldiers imagined life going on back at home and longed to be restored to their families, so this vision of a new order, reconciled to God, is offered to sustain us all and give us hope.

Guidelines

This week's readings have shown us how mission is intertwined with the need for reconciliation. God's mission of love to the world calls us to work for peace and justice among all people. Remembering the anniversary of the start of the World War I helps us to realise that this is not just a 'nice idea' but a mission imperative.

- Which of the readings this week inspired you most? What was it exactly that gripped your imagination?
- Imagine you were part of the Israelite communities hearing the words of any of these prophets. How do you think you might have reacted to them? Who are the modern prophets in our society and how do they communicate?
- Thinking about your church and your local situation, what one thing could you change or improve to show God's reconciling love more clearly to others?
- You might like to pray for all those situations where you know that people are in need of reconciliation—among friends, between family members, in your local community, in our country and between nations.

1 Prayer

Matthew 6:7–14

The Lord's Prayer is at the heart of Christian spirituality because Jesus gave it to us himself. His prayer enables us to focus on God and strengthens our personal spiritual resources, but at the same time it prepares us to be evangelists. We start with our relationship with God, the God we want to share—and this God is not just some abstract entity but is intimately connected to us. Jesus calls God 'Abba', 'Father' (v. 9), so here is the beginning of mission: we are God's children, loved and desired by him, and in that relationship we feel respect, honour and reverence toward him.

What do we expect to get from God's mission in and to the world, apart from this divine love? A world that is as God desires it: 'as it is in heaven' (v. 10). This is what we hope for, for all people and indeed the whole creation. What do we need to do to make it happen? We need to take care of our everyday needs (v. 11) and to maintain a right relationship between ourselves and other people (v. 12). Our care and forgiveness are both reflected in God's love and forgiveness poured out to us.

The Lord's Prayer also reminds us to pray that we are never subjected to evil (v. 13). This is a profoundly important part of our spiritual preparation for mission and evangelism. It is all too easy to be swayed by our own power, our selfish interests, and the need to bolster our self-esteem or even simply to convince ourselves of our own faith. That leads not to evangelism but to the possible spiritual abuse of others. On a larger scale, we should remember that, one hundred years ago, millions of people were caught up in an unimaginable evil and became subject to powers they could neither control nor sway. We need to give thanks for peace in our nations and to pray that we will never, unlike these previous generations, have to go through such evil times.

Jesus, too, lived at a time of tension and unrest under Roman occupation and was eventually arrested as a self-proclaimed 'king' who went against the power of Caesar. In giving us this prayer, he reminded us that we should always hope not to be brought to the time of trial but that, even so, it could happen. If we find ourselves in testing times, we will need our reserves of strength, faith and courage and trust in God.

2 Call

Matthew 4:18–22; John 1:35–42

Think of those famous World War I posters showing Lord Kitchener and the phrase 'Your country needs you'. Many young men were stirred to join up, some lying about their age, to defend their country, their homes and families and their way of life. They found the call irresistible and they went to the trenches believing that they were offering themselves in a great cause.

It's worth considering the contrast between this call-up and Jesus' call to the disciples in the Gospels of Matthew and John. Even though many would die for his cause also, his call came to the disciples in a different way. The disciples saw something in Jesus that opened up their horizons and personified their hopes. Jesus offered them more than a political cause: it was the chance to 'fish for people' (Matthew 4:19), and this fishing is not just the liberation of people from oppression but also the transformation of hearts and minds, bringing God back to the centre of people's lives. In other words, Jesus called the disciples to a mission spirituality: he invited them not just to live holy lives according to the religious law, but to understand and bring about an inward transformation, focused on what God wanted, not what they wanted. The success of this call also depended on people like Zebedee, who did not leave the nets but stayed behind, keeping his business going and making it possible for the others to follow Jesus. Everyone who contributes to what Jesus offers responds to the call in their own way; supporting is as important as doing.

For God's mission to be fulfilled, we all must respond to the sense of vocation, of call. Jesus is still calling us to follow him, because the mission of God that is present through the Holy Spirit in the world needs us to make the gospel real in people's lives. That call is not a demand for enlistment but a gracious invitation; it depends on our seeing in Jesus someone worth learning from and dedicating ourselves to. We become obedient to Christ, but, unlike the soldiers of World War I, we do not find ourselves subject to an impersonal authority. Instead, we are free to explore—free, if we choose, to say 'yes' to God's will for us.

3 Change

Acts 8:26–40

Looking back a hundred years, we can see that human beings have lived through the most incredible amount of change. Since World War I, demographics, territories, political landscapes, industry and attitudes have all changed. For many people, such change has not come about through choice; everyone has had to adapt and cope as well as they can. In the West, one particular change is a decline in churchgoing and traditional forms of Christian faith. Although we are still committed to God's mission, to become a Christian today and to live out that calling can be both countercultural and risky. In some cases, commitment to Christ in the UK today can separate a person from their culture and their family: it is a lonely and occasionally dangerous decision. Is it worthwhile?

The story of Philip and the Ethiopian eunuch should encourage us not to give up in mission and evangelism, because in Acts 8 we learn how God guides even unlikely people towards radical, life-affirming change. This story also highlights the way in which mission is linked to the spirituality not only of the person who becomes a Christian but also of the one who guides that person towards God.

It is not surprising that this reading is set in the context of a journey. Philip is spiritually open to the promptings of God, who sets his path to intersect with that of the eunuch at precisely the right time. Meanwhile, the eunuch has become intrigued by the scriptures and senses something here that will transform his life, but he needs Philip to unlock the meaning that will alter the course of his journey, both physically and spiritually. Through Philip, the eunuch hears about Jesus and the good news. Seeing the water, he asks Philip to help him make a leap of faith, to alter direction, to embrace change. The eunuch ventures into the unknown, but he knows he is not alone. He trusts Philip to help him begin his new life through baptism and he knows he will not be let down.

The way we manage change is therefore an important part of mission spirituality. With change comes challenge but also opportunity. If God brings us to intersect with the spiritual journeys of others, will we recognise the richness that is on offer there? Will we respond?

4 Harvest

John 4:31–42

The anniversary of the beginning of World War I this year reminds us that, like the Jews and Samaritans in this passage from John's Gospel, all human beings can find themselves on deeply entrenched opposing sides. What spiritual resources do we have that will break down those barriers? The answer is that a shared faith tradition can make a real difference. Even in the midst of fierce fighting, and especially at Christmas, combatants sometimes remembered that they were just human beings with families and loved ones. Yet, in the end, the harvest of the war was huge numbers of dead, friend and enemy alike.

Earlier in John 4, Jesus overcame the traditional enmity between Jew and Samaritan, asking a Samaritan woman for a drink (4:7). In today's reading, he talks about the results of healing the division between enemies. Such reconciling work does God's will, nourishing the participants and contributing to the harvest for eternal life, which is what ultimately matters. Here we see how he overcomes the suspicion and hostility between Samaritans and Jews, so that many Samaritans come to believe that he is the Messiah (vv. 39–42).

We also learn that the spiritual nourishment of mission gives us the energy we need to heal the world: 'My food is to do the will of him who sent me and to finish his work' (v. 34). Mission spirituality means seeing beyond an individual's background, faith, colour or gender to the person whom God desires to gather into the harvest. If this discernment of a common humanity was possible, at moments, even in the middle of a great war, how much more should we today be able to cultivate a missional spirituality that equips us to see Christ in others, and God at work in every person's life, no matter who they are or whose 'side' they are on?

Jesus doesn't just talk about 'the crop for eternal life' (v. 36). We see him actually enabling the creation of many new believers. In this passage, Jesus shows us how we should all be working for God's purposes, for a harvest not of the dead but of the living.

5 Sacrifice

John 15:12–17

Every Remembrance Day, we recall and give thanks to God for those who made the 'ultimate sacrifice' in giving their lives on the battlefield.

In John 15:13, Jesus too reminds us that to die for another person is the greatest act of love that any of us can perform. To give up our life, the most precious gift we have received from God, voluntarily, to save others is an extraordinary sacrifice. Sacrifice is an important part of the spirituality of mission because love for others overcomes the hatred and evil of human actions. When people see compassion and love at work, it can be an incredibly powerful witness.

Another significant part of today's reading is that Jesus reminds the disciples that they are bound to him and to each other by friendship, not by the obligations of a master–servant relationship. The spiritual context that allows a person to die in place of another depends on fellowship, love for a friend, a commitment to and interest in the preciousness of that person's life. This is not a call for heroics or even bravery; rather, self-sacrifice emerges as a consequence of a deep knowing of the other person as a friend and fellow human being. It comes from relationship and a feeling of connection, not out of a vacuum.

Of course, these words of Jesus are also prophetic, for he himself laid down his life for his friends, and for every single one of us. But because Jesus reminds us that the spiritual resources of friendship and sacrifice are connected with one another, we can be sure that his sacrifice also includes us. Jesus rose from the dead to show that obedience to his commandment of love for others undoes the hatred of the world; his resurrection confirms the victory of love over all the evil that led him to his crucifixion. Missional spirituality therefore springs from the command of Jesus to love others as we ourselves have been loved (v. 12), and to understand that part of that love is the willingness to sacrifice everything, even our lives, to bring peace and justice to the world.

6 Overcoming evil

Romans 12:9–21; 2 Corinthians 5:20

How do we cope with the aftermath of war? When we look at the loss of human life, the damage to property and businesses, and the pain and bereavement sorrow that follow in its wake, how can we not continue to feel anger and hatred and a desire for revenge towards the old enemy? These residual feelings are well known to us and continue to cause all kinds of problems in our communities—for example, when peace-loving Muslims are harassed or attacked because of acts of terrorism by extremists who have nothing to do with them at all.

In Romans 12, Paul tells us where to get the spiritual resources we need to overcome feelings of vengeance and fear. We must love, pray for and forgive our enemies, laying down all our negative feelings. We must learn to bless them, not curse them. Of course we must speak out against evil, but we must not succumb to it. Our job is to love others, whatever they have done, and not allow ourselves to be eaten up with thoughts of payback. It may be hard to turn away from entirely natural feelings of anger towards those who have hurt us, but Paul reminds us that God has the broadest perspective on human history, and everything that takes place in our world is subject to God's judgment. We do not need to try to work it all out from our small corner of time and space; our job is to do the best we can to love our enemies, because, in the end, that love will make us stronger and set us free.

These resources of love, peace-making, reconciliation and forgiveness, inspired in us by the Holy Spirit, are the qualities that equip us for mission. Through drawing on our capacity for friendship and compassion, we become ambassadors for Christ, reflecting his love for others (2 Corinthians 5:20). As a community, offering each other mutual support and encouragement, being devoted to one another and sharing each other's joy and pain, we can become powerful reconciling communities. Any church, then, is not just a group of fellow believers meeting together; it should be an active force in the world through which God acts and through which those acts of God can be clearly seen by others. In this way our work in mission and our Christian spirituality reinforce each other, giving us unique tools to overcome evil and replace its damage with love.

Guidelines

In this week's readings, we have looked at the relationship between mission and Christian spirituality. The background to the centenary of the start of World War I also shows us the contrast between the destructive power of human conflict and the creative, affirming invitation from Jesus to choose life and to follow him.

- Which of this week's readings has inspired you most? What was it about the reading that got your attention?

- What inner resources do you think we need in order to share our faith confidently with others?
- What one thing could you change in your local situation to encourage and strengthen the mission work of your church?
- You might like to pray for all those involved in mission, including any agencies that your church supports. You might also like to spend some time praying the Lord's Prayer and paying special attention to the words Jesus gave us.

FURTHER READING

Brian Castle, *Reconciling One and All*, SPCK, 2008.

Raymond Fung, *The Isaiah Vision*, WCC, 1992.

Kirsteen Kim (ed.), *Reconciling Mission: the Ministry of Healing and Reconciliation in the Church Worldwide*, ISPCK, 2005.

Kirsteen Kim and Andrew Anderson, *Edinburgh 2010: Mission Today and Tomorrow*, Regnum Edinburgh 2010 Series, Volume 3, 2011.

Anne Richards with the Mission Theology Advisory Group, *Unreconciled?* CTBI, 2010.

Mission Theology Advisory Group, *Transparencies: Pictures of Mission through Prayer and Reflection*, CHP, 2002.

Anne Richards with the Mission Theology Advisory Group, *Sense Making Faith*, CTBI, 2007.

Roger Helland and Leonard Hjalmarson, *Missional Spirituality: Embodying God's Love from the Inside Out*, IVP, 2011.

The Digital Archive for War Poetry at www.oucs.ox.ac.uk/ww1lit

Resources for exploring spirituality at www.spiritualjourneys.org.uk

Lamentations

Sadly, in the church in England today, we often fail to recognise the importance of sorrow and grief, particularly the importance of sorrow at our own sinfulness. Christians have much to learn from Lamentations, because it teaches us to respond properly to the consequences of our own sin, perhaps most especially when we are in the midst of the mess that has resulted from our selfishness and lack of trust in Jesus. What is more, Lamentations also helps us to recognise that sin is not an individual affair but always has wide-reaching consequences.

One way of understanding these consequences is to think in terms of a 'ripple effect'. Just as a stone dropped in a pond causes ripples to spread across the surface of the water, so the ripples of our sin travel out from ourselves and wash over more and more people. The bigger the sin, the bigger the ripples, and the more people are affected. Furthermore, whole societies can be caught up in sinful patterns and cycles. Lamentations has much to say on the subject of both individual and corporate sin—topics we may wish to avoid but ones that we ignore to our own loss.

Lamentations mourns the destruction of Jerusalem in 587BC by the Babylonians. For convenience I will assume that it was written by Jeremiah, although scholars do debate this point. Dobbs-Allsopp sums up the situation described in Lamentations like this: many people have been either killed (1:19; 2:20–21) or exiled (1:3, 5, 18), the temple has been desecrated and destroyed (1:10; 5:18), houses and public buildings are devastated (2:2, 5, 9), worship is disrupted (1:4), political power is in the hands of foreigners (1:5; 5:2), the Davidic line is ended (4:20) and the general population suffers famine (4:3–4, 9; 5:9). Yahweh appears to have abandoned his people (5:20). With everything so hopeless, is it any wonder that the result is a heartfelt, heart-rending lament? Read Jeremiah 7:1–15 and reflect on the false confidence that he castigates. What might Jeremiah have said if he were preaching in our day?

1 Suffering without God

Lamentations 1

Jerusalem the widow sits desolate in the ruins, weeping over her loss, mourning her destruction. The blackest of grief overwhelms her; waves of sorrow crash over her, drowning her in gloom. The worst of all is the fact that this sorrow is entirely of her own making. Jeremiah puts into words the agony of the exile, the pain of the destruction that followed Jerusalem's persistent and continuous rebellion against the living God.

The opening chapter of Lamentations paints a bleak picture. There is no one present to comfort or help Jerusalem (vv. 2, 7, 9, 16, 17, 21). Lamentations 1 is full of statements of reversal: Jerusalem has become what she never thought she would be. As the text unfolds, it becomes increasingly clear that God is responsible for inflicting the suffering that is being endured. There are appeals for God to see the devastation experienced by Jerusalem, then accusations against him, before complaints against old foes, acknowledgment of guilt and more desperate pleas for sympathetic engagement of some sort. The speaker's voice shifts between third-person narrative description of Jerusalem's woes and first-person lament as Jeremiah first describes the city's plight and then gives the city her own voice.

Deuteronomy 28:52–57 promises invasion, siege and destruction for constant sin against God and God's word, and verses 58–63 threaten affliction, depopulation and exile for the same reason. For Jeremiah's generation, these warnings have become a reality. It took a long time for Jerusalem to come to this position: at first she gave no thought to the future and carried on regardless, but she found herself trying to walk on air, and her fall was astounding as she plummeted to the depths. Now, bruised and battered, she cries out in pain.

Lamentations 1 does not really contain any hope of salvation: the pain of punishment is still too severe. This is an important lesson for us to learn as Christians—that at times God leaves us to suffer the consequences of our sins. Although it is right and proper for us to recognise that we are saved by grace through faith, it is also important that we do not belittle the reality of sin and its consequences. We are unlikely to experience devastation on the scale that Jerusalem endured; nevertheless, there is much food for thought here.

2 Looking for someone to blame

Lamentations 2

When things go wrong, our natural impulse is to search out those responsible in order that they might be publicly named and shamed. Sometimes this can be healthy and a just course of action. At other times it is little more than an emotional release as we avoid any possibility of personal culpability. In Lamentations 2, Jerusalem wrestles with these two positions, struggling to accept that her guilt is the ultimate cause of the punishment that Yahweh has visited upon her. The idea of God punishing his own people for their disobedience is one that the people of God, both then and now, have found difficult, but it is one that we need to take seriously if we are to keep our relationship with the Lord on an even keel.

Like chapter 1, Lamentations 2 is an acrostic poem, creating an intentionally thorough description of the punishment that God has brought upon Zion. There are three main sections in the chapter, each with a different voice. Jeremiah first gives third-person narrative details of Jerusalem's condition, describing the Lord's punishment of the city (vv. 1–10); he then reverts to first-person speech that describes Jerusalem's woes indirectly (vv. 11–12) and addresses her directly, counselling her to cry out to the Lord (vv. 13–19); third, Jerusalem herself responds by addressing Yahweh directly, asking him to see what has happened to her (vv. 20–22). The poem contains elements of dirge, lament and prophetic speech.

Do you give much thought to the consequences of sin? The people to whom Jeremiah preached had a false confidence in their status as the people of God. It would be easy for Christians to have a false confidence in the grace of God revealed to us in Jesus Christ. Is this a trap we fall into—the trap of assuming that God's grace means we can live as we like? Paul challenges this attitude in Romans 6, reminding us that, as Christians, we must be dead to sin but alive to God in Christ, living as slaves of righteousness. As he puts it and as Lamentations reminds us, 'the wages of sin is death,' but fortunately, for all who trust in God, 'the gift of God is eternal life in Christ Jesus our Lord' (Romans 6:23).

3 A glimmer of light

Lamentations 3:1–39

There's an old saying that the night is darkest before the dawn, and it is certainly true that the emotion in Lamentations goes down to the depths before there is even a brief glimmer of light and hope. Even that brief glimmer is faltering and feeble. The whole of Lamentations is a storm. Here we enter into the eye of that storm, where the wind seems calm and things are peaceful, or at least relatively peaceful compared with what rages on outside the eye. Perhaps the most encouraging thing is simply that the eye is the centre of the storm, which means we are halfway to the end.

Lamentations 3 has 22 sections, each of three lines, and each line in the section begins with the same letter. In verses 1–39 there are two voices; first an individual speaks of his own experience (vv. 1–24), then there is a switch to third-person masculine singular (vv. 25–39). These two voices correspond with two major topics: what one person has learnt through suffering, and a description of what it is good to do in such circumstances. Jeremiah announces that he has endured the pain that God sent for the city's sins, and that it has been almost too much to bear. He lists his suffering and hardships, making it clear that God is the source of it all. As his thoughts turn to the Lord, however, so his attitude turns to one of prayer. This is echoed in the shift in voice from verse 25 onward, where there is a reminder of the need to recognise Yahweh's goodness, to maintain a patient hope in him and to avoid all complaint.

This chapter contains the most famous part of Lamentations—indeed, probably the only part that most Christians know, even if they are unaware of its source (vv. 22–23). We must be careful to avoid divorcing it from the wider context. While we may love to sing that the Lord's mercies are new every morning and his faithfulness is great, it is also true that he is a just God who punishes wickedness, rebellion and sin. We must neither assume forgiveness nor try to earn it ourselves. Our own access to God's grace is through Jesus Christ, and we must come to him each and every day, asking for a fresh gift of his Spirit to enable us to live in a way that pleases him.

4 We cry out to the Lord

Lamentations 3:40–66

In the second section of chapter 3, the people speak together (vv. 40–47) before a return to the individual voice (vv. 48–66). Today's focus is all on prayer: there is an exhortation to community prayer and a prayer of confidence in the Lord. The section begins with a call to self-examination and repentance. It must be thorough and searching, beginning with the heart. It cannot remain internal but must be spoken out. There is a realism in this prayer: repentance may not lead to instant relief, as the consequences of sin must still be worked through.

The anguish of it all drives Jeremiah to tears (v. 48); as his beomes the sole voice, it is clear that he will continue weeping and interceding until God looks out of the windows of heaven, sees a repentant nation and responds with restoration. Jeremiah is clear that in the depths of his suffering, Yahweh is the only person he can turn to. He needs the Lord's reassurance and defence.

In the closing section, Jeremiah starts to use legal terminology (v. 58), suggesting that the Lord has become his lawyer, defending him against an unjust enemy. God has redeemed Jeremiah's life, renewing his confidence and bringing vengeance on his enemies.

In this chapter, hope has been kindled but the flame is burning only quietly at present. There has been repentance and a suggestion of a resolve to live differently, but it can hardly be described as a complete turnaround just yet. The focus is still on the punishment that Israel endures and there are suggestions that, even now, there is a danger of presuming too much of the Lord.

There is also a clear reminder of the need for us to admit our own sin and failure. Sometimes we need to repent publicly if we are to be truly forgiven and free. James reminds us of our need for heartfelt repentance

(James 4:7–10) and the importance of confessing our sins to each other (5:16). Sometimes it is simply not enough to say sorry to God: we must also confess to those we have wronged and, if necessary, make public restitution, just as Zacchaeus does, once his life has been transformed by Jesus (Luke 19:8). Furthermore, Lamentations 3 teaches us that even when we admit our guilt and begin to turn our lives around, the onward path may still be difficult and full of challenges.

5 Looking with fresh eyes

Lamentations 4

As we enter chapter 4, we have left behind the eye of the storm and are back in the full fury of the wind. Although the pressure is back on again, however, there is also some cause for hope, as we have left the harshest phase of the storm behind and now can look with fresh eyes. Chapter 4 parallels chapter 2 in depicting the devastation of Jerusalem, but there is one crucial difference. In this chapter the flower of hope is slowly beginning to develop; the hope is still only a bud, but, if nurtured, it will develop further.

The structure of the chapter can be outlined as follows: in the first speech (vv. 1–10), a voice from the community details the horrors Jerusalem has faced and continues to face; in the second (vv. 11–16), Jeremiah adds his depiction of the terrors Jerusalem has faced because of her sin; in the third (vv. 17–20), a speaker from the community describes the fall of the city, while in the fourth (vv. 21–22), a prophetic voice pronounces woe on Edom and relief for Jerusalem.

Jeremiah makes it clear that sin must be punished and that there must be an admission of guilt and heartfelt repentance before any possibility of restoration. In the Gospels, Jesus gives us much to think about that reinforces this understanding. At times, he tells parables suggesting that we will be judged on the basis of our actions, perhaps most strikingly in the parables of the talents and of the sheep and goats (Matthew 25:14–46). If we read only Lamentations and these parables out of the whole Bible, it would be easy to think that salvation was all about our own actions.

However, our relationship with God is precisely that—a relationship, not a working agreement. Lamentations reminds us to align our words with our actions and also to recognise that when we sin we are liable for punishment, and that the punishment for ignoring God is potentially very harsh. There is, of course, the continual possibility of repentance; even the thief on the cross managed to repent just before he died (Luke 23:40–43), but the message of Lamentations is that there comes a time when repentance is no longer possible, where the only available option is punishment.

6 The final chapter

Lamentations 5

Lamentations draws to a close, but there is still unfinished business. The work of repentance and restoration has begun but is by no means complete. This is the shortest and least well-structured acrostic of the poems, consisting of 22 one-line verses, with no strict alphabetic sequence. There is only one voice in this chapter: Jeremiah records a community lament as the people pray together. Verse 1 invokes divine remembrance, and verses 2–18 list the woes that the people have endured. The key interpretative problem comes at the end. Should verses 19–22 be seen as positive or negative? In other words, does Lamentations end on a note of hope or of despair? I would argue that it ends on a note of cautious optimism, with a fledgling hope that, in due time, the Lord will act to restore his people.

In these closing verses, Jeremiah strikes a hopeful yet uncertain note. Despite everything the people have endured, they have not lost their fundamental faith in Yahweh's absolute sovereignty. Although much of the book has been concerned with expressing their pain, the people have not abandoned trust in Yahweh. They still pray to him because, despite the overwhelming pressure to abandon their faith, they know that he is the only one worth relying on. The people are equally aware of their own finite nature. They are concerned that Yahweh has abandoned them for so long; they know they have broken the covenant and are suffering the consequences, but they also implore Yahweh to see they are no longer in rebellion. Since they are reforming their ways, cannot Yahweh return to what he was before their punishment began?

The people make a clear plea for restoration, then—a restoration not simply of their fortunes but of their relationship with Yahweh, their covenant partner. They confess their faith and firm belief that only Yahweh can bring about renewal of relationship: he is the wronged party in the covenant so he must be the one to decide to restore. This is not a question of divine sovereignty but of divine choice. The people have confessed and repented and now they wait in expectation—but they are still waiting. They have not yet received restoration. How much longer should they wait? How much more of Yahweh's anger should they endure? They know he will not be angry for ever, and so they wait on his timing.

Guidelines

The most difficult element of Lamentations is probably the lack of a 'happily ever after'. We expect a clear resolution, a solution, a positive ending, but Jeremiah doesn't offer us any of those. Instead we are left feeling almost let down, still unsure whether God really does care, and unclear as to when—or even if—he is going to act. If we reflect on our own experience, however, this uncertainty is probably much more true to life than any glib simple solution.

Things rarely turn out as we hope, and we are often left disappointed, wishing we had a clearer idea of when and how God was going to act. This is nowhere more painfully true than when we have sinned. A shattering destruction of the covenant such as that caused by Israel's adultery was never going to be easily healed. The restoration of relationship would be a long, slow, tentative process, as the people of God gradually became increasingly committed to a healthier, honest, true relationship with Yahweh.

Sometimes our return to the Lord may be swift and joyful, as in Jesus' story of the younger son coming to his senses and being taken back in by his father (Luke 15:11–32), but that story ends with the celebratory party the first night back. On the morning after, the slow process of re-establishing a relationship shattered by selfishness would begin in earnest. It would not be an easy or straightforward process, but it would be a necessary one. Lamentations records the tentative first steps as the people of God come to a realisation of their own need for repentance and call out to God for the restoration of relationship that only he can give. Let us hope and pray we never end up so far away from Yahweh that we also have to go through such a painful return to his grace, but even if we do, Lamentations reminds us that there is always a way back. The road may be long and hard and painful, but while we are still living, it is there and open for us to take.

FURTHER READING

Elie Assis, 'The Unity of the Book of Lamentations', *Catholic Biblical Quarterly* Vol. 71, 2009, pp. 306–329.

F.W. Dobbs-Allsopp, 'Tragedy, Tradition and Theology in the Book of Lamentations', *Journal for the Study of the Old Testament* Vol. 74, 1997, pp. 29–60.

Paul House, *Lamentations* (Word Biblical Commentary), Nelson, 2004.

Tom Wilson has written up his reflections on Lamentations in more detail under the title *Life in the Storm* (2011). It can be bought from www.lulu.com.

Isaiah 40—48

These chapters of Isaiah address the situation of the community that had been exiled from Judah to Babylon by the Babylonian King Nebuchadnezzar in 597 and 587BC (see 2 Kings 24—25). Babylon is mentioned more than once (see, for example, Isaiah 43:14; 47:1), and so is Cyrus the Persian, who defeated Babylon in 539BC and established the mighty Persian empire (see 44:28; 45:1). It looks, therefore, as though the situation presupposed is towards the end of the exilic period.

All of this took place more than 150 years after the time of the great prophet Isaiah himself, so most scholars maintain that these chapters were written by a different author. This does not mean, however, that they are completely detached from the first half of the book. Several major themes connect the two parts, and they cohere in the sense that Isaiah had anticipated deliverance after judgment and this prophet proclaims that the time of that deliverance has now dawned.

His initial message was evidently received with little enthusiasm. The people felt neglected and isolated, as though God no longer cared (see 40:27). The prophet's ministry as encapsulated in these chapters therefore concentrates very much on enlarging their understanding of God as Creator and Redeemer and on showing how they have an important role to play in his developing plans for the future.

In studying this material, we must be realistic about the fact that our understanding of creation and history will not allow us to take some of the short cuts that this prophet sometimes seems to take; we also need to keep in mind that the people of God are not now organised on a national basis. The underlying fact about God as Creator remains, however, so we should not be afraid of grappling with modern expressions of ancient truths. The chapters contain more than their fair share of famous 'quotes'; they must be read in their wider context if they are to act as anything more than cheap slogans.

Comments are based on the New Revised Standard Version of the Bible.

1 God is coming back

Isaiah 40:1–11

Before the prophet gets down to addressing the many problems that the exiled community in Babylon is facing, he introduces his message by giving the people a glimpse of the final outcome. He wants to lift their focus from wallowing in a dispirited sense of self-pity to a vision of how God can transform even hopeless-looking circumstances.

Several voices join to bring this word of encouragement. First, a group of messengers are to proclaim that the people can be freed from the shackles of past guilt (vv. 1–2). Looking back, there is now no impediment to the full restoration of God's special covenant with his people ('my people… your God': see Exodus 6:7; Jeremiah 31:33).

Second, a different voice announces that God is now returning to Zion from, as it has seemed to the people, his own exile from their land and sanctuary. No external barrier can stand in his way (vv. 3–5).

If we gather from verses 9–11 that his people are to accompany him on this journey (he leads and carries them like a shepherd), then they might well have protested that they did not feel up to so momentous a challenge (vv. 6–8). The answer to such human frailty, though, is 'the word of our God' (v. 8)—not, of course, the Bible, but that powerful word by which creation was brought into existence and which remains transformative. It is 'the good news that was announced to you', according to the explanation of this passage in 1 Peter 1:23–25.

So the new beginning for the people is wholly dependent on their involvement in what God is doing. Past guilt and future mountainous problems cannot stand in his way or theirs, and the outcome will reach far beyond their own circle: God's glory will be acknowledged universally (v. 5). It is visionary, yes, but not unrealistic, then or now, for a responsive and dependent people of God. But how to get there from the unpromising present? The following chapters seek to engage realistically with the despair of the present, which threatens to inhibit even the first step on the journey.

2 Have you not heard?

Isaiah 40:21–31

We have all heard sermons like it! After singing a hymn about some important doctrinal point or including an affirmation of active commitment, the preacher looks around the languid congregation and asks, 'Well, you have just sung it; don't you believe it?' or words to that effect.

The exilic community in Babylon was not just languid; it had more or less given up on God altogether. He did not seem to answer the people's prayers or even show an interest in their condition. They might do better to follow the gods of Babylon. Verse 27 shows a mixture of resentment and despair in their attitude.

To counteract this, the prophet begins in these chapters to marshal a series of arguments to show that God is both capable and willing to move powerfully in restoration. He is the Creator, he controls the great flow of history, and he will be as faithful to his promises of future deliverance as he was to his past warnings of judgment for sin.

Verses 21–23 sound very much like some of the psalms that praise God as Creator. No doubt the exiles continued to use these songs in their weekly worship, and they would probably have admitted their truth even if they could not apply them to their present situation. The prophet picks up on this starting-point rather like a preacher, but with great skill that preachers would do well to emulate. He proceeds by way of a series of questions to secure agreement that if God is the creator and sustainer of the world, he is also well able to sustain the faint, the weary and the powerless. This does not mean that he automatically will sustain them, but those who wait upon him expectantly in this belief will find that their despair is changed to soaring hope.

In today's world, where our understanding of the process of creation is far more sophisticated, it might be easy to dismiss this approach as naïve or outdated. Christian testimony refutes this facile rejection, however. Precisely by prayerful meditation on the vastness of the created order and the one whose 'understanding is unsearchable' (v. 28), we learn to see our own weariness in a different light and a truer perspective. It does not belittle our frustrations but it helps us in turn to 'renew our strength' in the life of faith.

3 God and the gods

When things are going badly, there is always a temptation to think that the grass is greener elsewhere. The community had been in exile for something like 50 years by this point. Might the propaganda therefore be true? It was in the name of his god Marduk that Nebuchadnezzar had destroyed Jerusalem and taken the leaders into exile. Their own God had done nothing to change their situation in the meantime, so maybe it was true that Marduk and his fellow gods were more powerful after all.

To counter such reasoning, the prophet takes his readers metaphorically to court. There are several passages like today's that use this device (see also 41:1–5; 43:8–13, for instance). Witnesses are summoned and each side is invited to put its case to the court.

The ground on which God chooses to argue his case is the control of history, whether past or future. The gods are mocked satirically; they can neither say nor do anything. He, by contrast, has foretold and already begun to act in an unprecedented manner. The 'one from the north' (v. 25) is undoubtedly the Persian Cyrus, whose rise to power was meteoric. He has not yet reached Babylon, but he will. What matters for now, however, is that God is putting down a marker here, in advance of the event, so that in retrospect it will be clear that even the affairs of international imperial policy are not outside his control. Unlike the other gods (vv. 28–29), God's word is seen to be effective.

It is only with hindsight that such claims can ultimately be tested, and history is littered with mad predictions that have proved to be illusory. What God declares here, however, is his faithful adherence to principles that have been stated long ago. These concern not only the justice of his judgment on Jerusalem, long anticipated by the earlier prophets ('the former things', v. 22), but also the promise of deliverance that he is now starting to reveal, if only the court has the eyes to see it. Such consistency of purpose is evident, too, in the longer history of our salvation, culminating in the work of Christ. This should encourage us in turn to see with hindsight that, regardless of hopeless-looking circumstances, God's ultimate control remains personal and self-consistent.

4 Here is my servant

Isaiah 42:1–4

God's 'servant' has already been mentioned by the prophet in Isaiah 41:8–10, and there too he is 'chosen' and 'upheld', so he must be the same character as we meet here. However, there he was called Israel/Jacob (probably meaning the whole of the exiled Judean community), whereas in chapter 42 it looks at first as though he is an individual. This is a famous conundrum on which scholars hold different opinions.

An important point to notice is that the only kind of character of whom all the things mentioned here are true is the king. Some of the features are also true of priests or prophets, but only of the kings is every one mentioned elsewhere in the Old Testament, so this must be a royal character. In Isaiah 55:3 we find that the promises once made to King David seem somehow to be transferred to a plural 'you', as though the people as a whole take over the role of David. That would work very well in today's reading. Just as previously David has been responsible for justice for his people, so now the people, at least ideally, are responsible for bringing justice to the wider world of the nations. As this idea is repeated three times (in vv. 1, 3 and 4), it is obviously the main point of the passage. So we have the depiction of a role that God always wants to be undertaken—the bringing of justice. The one who fulfils this role, however, and the circle of people among whom he works, may vary according to changing historical circumstances.

Another variation is that, unlike earlier kings, this one will work almost incognito. In today's world, those most in need of justice—the 'bruised reeds' and 'dimly burning wicks'—do not want exposure to media intrusion and political publicity, which only exploit deprivation to further their own agendas. The people of God in any age should take note as well: although it may take considerable endurance (v. 4), our aim should be to serve those in need, not to undertake something simply to advance our own interests. In this, too, Jesus provides the model of servanthood (see Matthew 12:15–21). If we want to say that he fulfilled this passage, as we surely can, this does not mean he exhausted its potential but rather that he set a pattern of fulfilment which his followers should seek to emulate.

5 Fear not

Isaiah 43:1–7

We have already seen examples of how the prophet tries to goad his audience into a lively faith that will enable them to face a new future with confidence and expectation. He has pointed them to God's power as Creator, his control of history and his faithfulness to his word. If we may allow ourselves to be a little imaginative, we can almost hear him interacting with the community's worship as he responds in different ways to their chanting of psalms and recitation of prayers.

Having delivered such a challenging message, the prophet may then have encountered a different sort of objection: even if we believe all that about God, what you are asking us to do is too much for us. The prospect of uprooting from our homes here in Babylon, with which we are at least familiar, to face an arduous journey into the unknown is more than we can bear. In the language of other passages, we feel crushed, poor and needy (41:17), a mere worm (41:14) who is incapable of facing up to the challenge.

In the manner of priests of old, the prophet brings words of personal reassurance, grouped under the banner that runs throughout scripture: 'Fear not!' More than that, he gives reasons, stretching throughout these verses with a compassionate note that we have hardly met before. In a jumble of images that encompasses protection against every foreseeable danger, the swapping of other nations for Israel as a fair ransom price, the presence of God in their midst as he assures them of his love, and the gathering in of other scattered or dispersed members of their wider community, the prophet seems to spare no pains in breathing a spirit of reassurance.

There is a balance in his ministry, therefore, which provides a good model for current spiritual leadership. While some want the prophetic proclamation of justice in the face of oppression, others seek to impart a spineless form of 'comfort' that is lacking in substance. We find here, by contrast, not a focus on one side or the other alone, still less an attempt to stir both together into a meaningless brew. Rather, the challenge remains undimmed even as the personal cost is addressed with tender understanding. The God who created you is simultaneously the God who redeemed you.

6 Satire against idols

Isaiah 44:9–20

One of the strongest means of political comment comes in the form of cartoons. When perhaps we have become bored rigid with endless talk, a cartoon may cut right through to the main point at issue and, moreover, be devastatingly effective because of its memorable humour. Of course it exaggerates, both in its pictorial portrayal and in its caption, but that is an accepted 'given' of the format.

There are several ways in which this passage might be compared to a cartoon. It too exaggerates: nobody could ever seriously entertain the logic of verses 14–17, for instance. Moreover, it is a misrepresentation of idolatry to suppose that those who made or worshipped idols ever thought in such crudely materialistic terms. The picture is effective, however, because it brings us face to face with the distinction in humankind between creator and created.

Along with other shorter passages of this kind (see 40:19–20; 41:6–7; 46:5–7), we encounter here a new voice in the Old Testament, one that affirms not simply that the God of Israel is the greatest of the gods but that in fact he is the only God and all others are a mere 'block of wood… a fraud' (vv. 19–20). Of course, along with this goes the idea that he must also therefore be the God of all nations, not exclusively of Israel. This may help to explain some of the universal elements that we have found in these chapters of Isaiah: they follow from the insight that he is the Creator of all. It also carries the consequence that Israel should be a witness and a servant of others; her knowledge has been given to her representatively and she therefore has a responsibility to share it generously.

In today's world, materialism of a rather different sort may be said to have become the new idol of Western civilisation (to go no further). We have become so used to it that we run the risk of lacking 'discernment' (v. 19) about its dangers. If ecclesiastical talk has dulled our senses, perhaps only a cartoon has the power to restore our sensitivity to the transcendent.

Guidelines

The passages we have read include some of the loftiest doctrinal assertions in the Old Testament, but they were addressed to a group of people who seem to have been spiritually depressed. At the same time, therefore, we have seen a tenderness in applying all this at the individual level, as well as the challenge to put it to the service of others who may be broken or in danger of being extinguished.

Reflect first on the links between your faith as expressed in church services and the realities of the daily grind (if such it be) at other times. Does the vision of the one empower and succour the other?

Beyond that, are there practical ways in which we as individuals or as local congregations can translate the comfort we have found into the just service of others in need, whom we meet in person or through the media?

You might find that meditation on Isaiah 42:8–9 could helpfully lead into prayer.

30 June–6 July

1 A relentless logic

Isaiah 44:24–28

This passage opens a new and dramatic section in the book in which God announces that he is about to use Cyrus, a Persian king who is still only on the rise, to effect his will. What is more, this king is going to be spoken of in the most positive of terms, even though he has had no previous contact with the community of God's people or any conscious dealings with God himself.

It is not difficult to imagine the response in some quarters if such a proposal were to be put forward today. Consequently, the prophet proceeds with some care in order to ground his announcement in a theological manner that will carry his audience. The argument moves steadily from God as the creator of the cosmos as well as the individual (once again the agreed starting point: see v. 24) through to the consequential power of his word, which overturns the plans of those who would oppose him and his people (an astute move to gain support) but which upholds the words of his servant (Isaiah and the present prophet). This leads to the immediate prediction that Jerusalem will be restored (again a vote-winner), and only then is Cyrus as his agent revealed, by which time it may be supposed that all opposition has been silenced.

I have deliberately phrased this provocatively, of course, but even so there can be no denying that the prophet has thought through carefully how best to present his God-given case. The Gospel saying about being as wise as serpents comes to mind (Matthew 10:16). Although there is much about 'church politics' that is abhorrent, there need be no shame in stretching our minds to prepare a well-grounded argument, based on first theological principles, when it is appropriate to do so. We are encouraged as Christians to have our minds transformed and renewed (Romans 12:2), not bypassed or sidelined. It would be a tragedy to miss out on the possibility of some new insight or development simply because our minds are closed to new insights in principle (even though, of course, we are not to accept change merely for change's sake: see 1 Timothy 4:1; 2 Timothy 4:2–3).

2 Cyrus, God's anointed

Isaiah 45:1–8

According to Cyrus's own account, he was welcomed into Babylon in the name of the Babylonian god Marduk because the last of the Babylonian kings, Nabonidus, had made himself unpopular with the local priests. He had taken himself off to a remote desert oasis for religious purposes, which meant neglecting his duties back home. In gratitude for his welcome, Cyrus allowed a number of the local sanctuaries to be restored.

We know all this from the Cyrus Cylinder, a famous text that some have hailed as the world's first statement of human rights. It is nothing of the sort, but it is interesting to see how it compares and contrasts with today's passage from Isaiah. Two relevant facts stand out. First, unusually for the ancient world, the Babylonians had allowed the exiled communities to live together and thus to retain their identities. This was unprecedented and, we may think, providential. Second, it is a fact that, for reasons of his own, relating to the control of his empire, Cyrus did permit some of the Judean exiles to return to Jerusalem, as recorded in the book of Ezra.

Although Cyrus knew nothing of the God of Israel (v. 4), that did not mean that God could not use him. He is even called 'anointed' (v. 1), the word from which we get 'messiah'. This certainly stretches our comprehension, but, with an echo of the longer passage that starts in 44:24, God claims at the end of verse 7 to be the one who does 'all these things'. That includes forming 'light and darkness', 'weal and woe'—not moral good and evil, but prosperity or disaster of any sort that may strike quite independently of our own personal causation.

The prophet encourages his hearers, and us through them, to be less restricted in their understanding of God and more open to acknowledge the freedom of his action even when it operates through other than expected channels. We do well to bear this in mind as we watch the development of global affairs, perhaps especially when we have difficulty in comprehending at the moment how it all fits together. Even Cyrus could be called anointed.

3 A God who hides himself

Isaiah 45:9–17

It is not surprising that some people, at least, must have replied to the prophet that the things he was announcing were quite impossible. We can imagine them protesting, 'God doesn't work like that. It does not conform to my understanding of what is just and righteous; I know better than you.'

The response in verses 9–11 is a stinging rebuke. The rhetorical questions point up the absurdity of thinking that we can tell God how he ought to behave. Once again, we then return to the theme that God's use of Cyrus is in line with his sovereignty as Creator. It is doubtful whether the objectors were satisfied at the time but, with hindsight, we can certainly agree that, as the old hymn puts it, 'God is working his purpose out'. Even if it takes years to come to a point of understanding, a dose of humility in the interim is becoming.

Beyond that, however, the second half of our passage brings us back to the point of the relevance of all this for the nations other than Israel. Note that the kind of universalism espoused by this prophet is far from the warm but flabby liberalism of a previous generation: these nations come in chains with their tribute and prostrate themselves to the unexpectedly restored Israel (v. 14). More important than their political circumstances, however, is their confession that they cannot see God for themselves, because he hides himself. At the same time, they confess that they can see what he has done for his people, so their witness will lead to an acknowledgment of the reality of their God and the futility of idols.

There can be no doubt that verses 14–17 are somewhat disjointed, and this may reflect complications in the way the text developed over time rather than being written at one sitting. Regardless of that discussion, however, it is also clear that there is no other witness available to the nations than the nation of Israel, which has been unexpectedly saved. Should the attitude of this restored community of Israel not be, therefore, to accept what God has done, despite its challenges to their previous worldview? If they continue in unbelieving criticism, it is the enslaved nations who will suffer.

4 Who carries whom?

Isaiah 46:1–7

We have already seen that this prophet is a master craftsman in his use of language, and this passage is no exception. Bel, a title for Marduk, and Nebo, his son, were two of the most important Babylonian deities. One job of the gods ought to be to support, to 'carry', their people. With the fall of Babylon to Cyrus, however, the prophet depicts the idols being themselves ignominiously carried away into captivity by weary pack-animals. The fact that, in the event, Cyrus did not banish the Babylonians into exile does not empty the picture of its irony; the gods suffer the fate from which they cannot deliver their people.

By contrast, the God of Israel is the one who always has carried, and always will carry, his people, even though they are the ones who, in fact, have been in exile. On this occasion, quite unlike in the previous chapter, the phrasing becomes intimate and tender: the carrying started 'from your birth' (v. 3) and will continue 'to your old age' (v. 4), and it is integrated into the sequence of divine activity that we have met repeatedly in earlier chapters: 'made… bear… carry… save' (v. 4).

Finally, in verses 5–7 the same theme is employed effectively in a resumption of the satirical polemic against idols and their manufacturers, who have to 'carry' the new idol to its position in a sanctuary (v. 7).

It is difficult sometimes to know whether to laugh or cry. Nobody could read this passage without a smile on their lips and we might be tempted to think that the prophet is just being clever again at the expense of idols and their devotees. The heart of the passage, verses 3–4, strikes a different chord, however. As an associate of his fellow exiles, the prophet knows that circumstances have brought them to the point of despair, where they cannot see why they were born, their future bespeaks only more travail, and his message beggars their belief. Into this circle of despondency he brings a personal word of comfort and reassurance, which is empowered by its comic sense of contrast with the fate of their oppressors. Behind all the rhetoric, a heart of passionate pastoral concern is pounding.

5 Former things and new things

Isaiah 48:1–11

After a chapter reflecting on the fall of Babylon (Isaiah 47), the prophet returns to address his primary audience of Jacob/Israel as he begins to move towards the mini-climax at the end of chapter 48. We are going to find there a call for radical action, and so, if the people are to respond positively to the call, they will need to be assured in their own mind that they are doing so for good reason.

He has already advanced a whole battery of theological arguments, as we have seen. That is fine as far as it goes, but something more is needed—trust as opposed to mere belief. It is one thing to say you believe that God is Creator; it is quite another to trust him when he commands you to leave home for an uncertain future.

To help encourage this trust, the prophet reminds his listeners that, in the past, God announced 'the former things' to them (vv. 3–5) so that when those events actually happened, people would know that God had done it. The problem for us is to know how to identify what the 'former things' were. They have been mentioned several times before and in some places it is obvious what is meant. In 43:16–18, for instance, there is a clear reference to the crossing of the Red Sea after the exodus.

In today's passage the reference is less obvious, but it would be attractive, as we read the completed book of Isaiah, to suppose that it refers to the predicted fall of Jerusalem to the Babylonians (as also at 41:22). That at least has had a major impact on the circumstances of the exilic community. Given God's good credentials, therefore, it would be only reasonable for them now to trust in the truthfulness of the 'new things' that he is declaring to them and so to act on that basis (vv. 6–8).

There is only one snag in that argument, which is the question of whether the one who is announcing what the new things are—the prophet—has got it right. The question is left unresolved in the book of Isaiah, but ultimately it was resolved by the fact that the Word was itself incarnated in the person of the prophet, Jesus. Where message and messenger are thus united, trust is made possible.

6 Get moving

Isaiah 48:17–22

Within the large and interconnected section of Isaiah that embraces chapters 40 to 55, there is an obvious division at the end of chapter 48. Several of the features we have studied in the previous chapters fall away from view in chapters 49—55 and some new features take their place. The oddly placed and isolated verse 22 at the end of chapter 48 seems to have been borrowed from 57:21, where it is more suitable to its context. Interestingly, this has the effect of dividing chapters 40—66 into equal thirds, suggesting that an editor in antiquity was perfectly well aware of how to flag up particular literary arrangements.

Not inappropriately, therefore, we reach a climax here with the command to 'go out… and flee' from Babylon (v. 20). Equally, as with every divine command, it is well grounded with promises and incentives. Some explicitly take up and reinforce elements from the previous chapters, such as the promise to accompany and provide for the people on their journey, just as their ancestors had experienced on the journey through the wilderness from Egypt to the promised land. Other incentives, only lightly introduced before, now receive greater attention: the failure to heed previous commands, leading to a hiatus in progress towards the realisation of the promises to Abraham, is a striking example (vv. 18–19).

Best of all, however, is the anticipated shout of joy that should accompany the people's departure (v. 20). This sounds like an outburst of praise that we might find in psalms, and it has also occurred before (see 42:10–12; 44:23). To praise God for what he has done, before it has happened, is an indication of complete trust in his faithfulness. Here, however, it goes a step further, because this praise will serve also as a proclamation to 'the end of the earth' that the Lord has redeemed his people. It serves well as a final reminder that redemption is not just something for smug personal enjoyment. The reality of its experience must spill over into proclamation. The water that gushed from the rock (v. 21) is an image as much as a physical reality.

Guidelines

The juxtaposition of a claim that God has providentially organised the imperialistic conquests of the pagan king Cyrus with a promise to carry his people 'even when you turn grey' (46:4) is breathtaking. Preachers seem often to err to one side or the other of this spectrum; do you? You might want to discuss this with a friend or spiritual counsellor.

Meditate prayerfully on Psalm 8:3–4 and Matthew 10:29–31 and then reflect on your own appreciation of God as creator, redeemer and sustainer.

A prayer by William of St Thierry (about 1080–1148):

Have mercy on us, Lord, have mercy.
You are the potter and we are the clay.
Somehow or other we have held together until now.
We are still carried by your mighty hand
and we are still clinging to your three fingers,
Faith, Hope, and Charity,

with which you support the whole great bulk of the earth,
that is to say, the whole weight of your people.
Cleanse our reins and hearts by the fire
of your Holy Spirit and establish the work
that you have wrought in us, lest we return
again to clay and nothingness.

FURTHER READING

Richard J. Clifford, *Fair Spoken and Persuading: An Interpretation of Second Isaiah*, Paulist Press, 1984.

John Goldingay, *The Message of Isaiah 40—55: A Literary–Theological Commentary*, T&T Clark, 2005.

Claus Westermann, *Isaiah 40—66: A Commentary*, SCM, 1969.

Hope and community

How do God's people respond to the call of God upon their lives, and what lessons can we learn about our missional calling today? What tools do we, as the people of God, need in order to offer hope to our communities in words and actions? The Bible is a book of encounter. It speaks of a God who created the world and developed deep relationships with humanity. It tells of moments of defiance when people turned away from God, but it also tells of transformative and redemptive encounters between God and humankind.

This week of studies takes seriously the church's call to be intentionally engaging with our identity as people in relationship with God. From the outset, there is a recognition that mission in the UK today can be a difficult calling, but throughout the notes, we draw on biblical stories of encounter that demonstrate how hope can be shown and discovered in our encounters with God and with other people.

Quotations are taken from the New International Version.

7–13 July

1 Singing songs in strange places

Psalm 137

God's chosen people find themselves in a strange land. They have been exiled from their homes and forcibly placed under a new regime. They have lost their power, their influence, their identity and, in some cases, their families and friends. This is a transient community now being forced to live with the sadness of remembering a past life. They are prisoners of conflict, transported into captivity.

The Hebrew people sit by the river and nostalgically remember better times. Their tears mix with the water of the river as they think of good times of prosperity and celebration. Together, they vow never to forget Jerusalem and all that the city meant for them, politically, socially and in terms of their religious beliefs.

Even as the Israelites remember and ponder the past, they are taunted by their captors, who jeer at them with requests for songs of hope and joy. For God's people, however, the songs of Zion are not the melody of their melancholy, and they hang their harps from the willow trees near their resting place.

The hope and promise that Jerusalem offered—of a place where the community of God could be together in God's presence—was not easily forgotten. Once removed to the strange land of Babylon, with the full realisation of what they had lost, the memory of God's presence and blessing upon his people became a powerfully binding narrative for them. In the midst of a changing landscape, God's people began to restore their worship and relationship with God, prioritising that relationship as a community. They narrated their history and, in so doing, reclaimed their identity as God's people. In Babylon, they would tell and sing a different narrative—one of God's redemption, care and provision.

Being surrounded by the taunts and temptations of an alien place and ideology could have led the Israelite people to an anaesthetised faith. Instead, through shared experience, storytelling and the pain of mourning and grief, they were able to hold to the hope that they would one day be reunited with one another in Jerusalem, their relationship with God restored.

The hope of this community is demonstrated in their resilience as they share the bitterness of national trauma, but also in their remembrance of God's goodness in the past and the promise that restoration, redemption and relationship might once again be an experienced reality.

2 Taking time

Ecclesiastes 3:1–14

This passage in Ecclesiastes is well known, not least due to the 1965 hit by the US folk-rock band The Byrds. Their lilting rendition of 'Turn! Turn! Turn!' was noted by one critic at the time as being 'folk rock's highest possible grace note'. It is a challenge to us to see this powerful poem not as a melancholic song of despair and meaninglessness, but as an invitation to note grace through lived experience.

God has 'made everything beautiful in its time' (v. 11) and has thus ordained life to have purpose, order, direction and meaning. It is God who holds everything in its course and attends to the needs of humanity in their right time and place. This is a significant message of hope for God's people as they seek to work out where they might best find God's grace in the midst of the terror and trauma of life. God's work is not slapdash or arbitrary; instead, he maintains a dynamic relationship with the created order.

Verses 1–8 have a musical quality, embodying through the rhythm of the poetry the waxing and waning of the experiences it describes. There is an inevitability to the changes of life, but, for the writer, this is not a threat to his belief in the existence of God; rather, it is a challenge to appreciate the kaleidoscope of life, each twist and turn bringing with it another refraction of God's kingdom.

The gift of God is that we may find satisfaction in each season of life—through work and through relationship—and that we may enable others to find (as the music critic noted) the 'grace notes' in their own experience. It is God who knows the overall purpose of events and emotions; it is the calling of the whole of humanity to respond. Our hope comes as we recognise the pattern and rhythm of life, taking the opportunity to live and work with the physicality and psychology of each moment. Life in all its fullness includes living, loving and working within the fragility and difficulty of human experience as well as seeking the coming kingdom of God, recognising that 'he has also set eternity in the human heart' (v. 11).

The challenge for us today is to have courage to notice the 'time' of life that we are currently experiencing, and to respond appropriately both to God and to the wider world.

3 Celebrity status

Matthew 18:1–5

'Who is the greatest?' is the question animating the disciples at the start of this passage. It would be easy to caricature their argument and to judge them for even contemplating a hierarchy of discipleship, but we must not forget that the question of who or what is the most important is a question that faces people every day.

It is no surprise, therefore, that Jesus challenges the tussling of the disciples with a reminder about the topsy-turvy nature of the kingdom of God. Those who are 'greatest' are held in esteem in community groups, and the 'greatest' person is often the fastest, smartest, wisest or oldest in the group. In the kingdom of God, however, Jesus demonstrates that to be the greatest is the privilege of those in society who are dependent on other people and on God.

Jesus does not succumb to the temptation of judging a Simon Cowell-style talent contest among the twelve disciples. Instead, he notices the context and calls a child towards him. This child becomes the latest sign of the kingdom, and, presented in the midst of the disciples, personifies the lesson.

The lesson is not a simplistic one, however. Jesus is not saying that children are the sole inheritors of the kingdom of heaven. He goes further than this, saying that anyone who wants to inherit the kingdom needs to become 'like' a child. The marks of discipleship are dependence on the Father, humility and constant learning. The faithful disciples are those who know their lowly status and are not afraid of asking questions. The lifelong task of a follower of Jesus is to wrestle with the temptation to pursue importance and pride and, instead, to live in humility with the calling to follow Christ.

It is apt that a God who entered the world as a child demands of the church the willingness to recognise his kingdom through the least in society. It is often at the margins of our communities, among the lowly, forgotten and marginalised, that hope and the kingdom of God can be most profoundly experienced. Jesus points out that by inviting these 'greatest' into fellowship with us, our communities are actually entertaining Christ. This is a sobering thought when we consider the people we eat with and invite into our homes. Dare we entertain Christ with us?

4 Receiving the gifts of others

Luke 7:36–39, 44–50

When it comes to offering hope to the communities in which we reside, it is all too easy to believe that we have all the tools and resources and that our job in mission is to solve the problems and provide for the needs of the people around us.

Again, the Bible indicates that there is a pattern of inversion to grace. It is not always the faithful follower of Jesus who is the one in receipt of the gift of grace. Sometimes, the glimpse of grace demands a willingness and ability to receive the gifts of others towards us and to empower others in their own response to Jesus.

Whereas Simon the Pharisee berates the woman for the extravagance and awkwardness of her aromatic offering to Jesus, Jesus notices the extraordinary gift that she is demonstrating, not just financially but also in terms of her repentance. The intimacy of her gestures could well have made the disciples nervous: they certainly go beyond the norms of recommended safeguarding pastoral practice. Jesus, however, does not flinch at the smashed pot, the expensive perfume, the hair draping or the kissing of his feet.

There are three responses to be noted in this passage: the disgust and shock of the onlookers; the compassion of the woman, washing the filthy feet of Jesus when no one else had done so; and the willingness of Jesus to receive such attention from a 'sinner'.

Jesus does not let the woman leave with the stinging words of the onlookers ringing in her ears. Although they have categorically asserted that she is a 'sinner' (by which they possibly meant 'prostitute'), Jesus transforms the situation, offers her forgiveness and sends her on her way.

Hope is a multisensory experience. The woman hoped for some of Jesus' attention and received absolution for her sins. Jesus was recognised as the Messiah and was anointed for his task by a woman of bad reputation with a clay jar of expensive ointment. As the contents were splashed over the room, the aroma of grace rose up. A simple act of love and compassion offered an opportunity to notice grace and to offer hope.

In offering Christ today to our communities, are we as willing as Jesus is here to accept the simple acts of multisensory love and kindness that are shown to us? Dare we notice the gifts of others as the beginning of a response to the generosity of Christ?

5 Hearing the right question

Acts 17:16–34

In a changing and challenging world, it can be tempting to withdraw from engagement with the materials and ideologies within it, for fear of becoming tainted or less-than-holy as a result. This was just as true for Paul, meeting the Greeks in Athens, as it is for us today.

Walking around the strange city, he was surrounded by statues dedicated to pagan gods. The Athenians were pluralistic in their belief structures: they were people of great intellect and loved nothing better than to hear the latest ideas from around the world. However, his initial culture shock soon became the catalyst for meeting with various city groups, including Stoics and Epicureans, and his philosophical reasoning was so impressive that he was invited to speak to bigger audiences.

Due to Paul's ability to gain credibility in his reasoning, the main philosophers of the city wanted to speak with him. Because of his ability to notice the messages written into the very fabric of the city (in statues and the work of poets), he was able to begin to speak directly into the longings of the Athenian people. Due to his confidence in the redemptive and universal power of the Spirit to bring about conversion, he communicated the gospel directly, and saw people meeting with Jesus as a result.

How often do we notice the things written into the fabric of the world in which we live, and use them to speak into the experience of the people we are meeting? For Paul, the gospel message was applied and transformative, speaking directly into the key areas of life for his listeners, leading them to an encounter with Jesus or, at least, piquing their interest. The gospel, in Paul's day, was not confined to Jews or to the synagogue; today, it is not confined to Christians or the church. To bring hope into our communities, we need to be willing to engage directly with the material of the cultures in which we live and breathe, to be familiar with the ideas, the monuments, the poets and the key messengers of our time. By listening to the influencers, a message of hope can speak directly into the deepest longing of communities, and bring encounters that renew and revitalise the church.

Sharing the gospel and engaging with a strange culture is not without its difficulties, of course, and Paul met a number of objections to his message. Noticing the key questions within a society does not guarantee a sympathetic hearing from those with power.

6 A question of character

Colossians 3:12–14

In a series of notes on hope and the community, it is important to end with a reminder about our own identity in Christ. If we are to offer hope to others, we need to be assured of our own place and vocation.

To another community, this one in Colosse, Paul speaks to encourage a group of people who have been able to build a church in difficult circumstances. They have had their fair share of difficulties, but Paul commends them for their faithfulness and their willingness to act prophetically in order to share the kingdom through their actions and personalities as well as their words.

The tools and resources that the Colossians have are the gifts of grace: they are to be people who know that they are fashioned and clothed in good character. Their actions stem from their sense of self-identity and the spiritual gifts of compassion, kindness, humility, gentleness and patience. The way that they act and the attitude that they hold towards others spring out of their relationship to Christ.

Paul assures them that they are 'dearly loved', which becomes the benchmark for their own loving service towards other people. The greatest virtue is love, which binds and influences all of the other gifts and graces within this passage.

The tools of mission and ministry, for the Colossian church, were not to be found only in deep philosophical arguments or in the right words spoken to a large group of people. Paul demonstrates here that the unity of the whole church is found in individuals of good character building a community of intentionally good character. Together, people grow in virtue and holiness and offer forgiveness to all who need hope and reconciliation.

Hope in community is about being the right person bringing the right message at the right time for the right recipient. It is not always about having a compelling argument or appearing to have all the answers. Confidence in the gospel is also to be found in developing the habits of a holy life and acting from a place of deep confidence in Christ, practising the fruit of the Spirit. This fruit is the fuel for action and engagement, which enable encounters with God in very different ways as people's physical and emotional needs are met.

Guidelines

We live in a world that is ever-changing and complicated. Throughout our day, we engage with people and products from around the globe and are affected, consciously and subconsciously, by issues and decisions over which we have little control. The places where we live, our local communities and our place on the world stage can often encourage us to retreat and disengage. We depend on like-minded friends and colleagues and begin to shut ourselves off from those who may be different from us.

In these tempestuous times, however, we must remember that God sent his Son, Jesus Christ, into this very world. The incarnation speaks of a God who loved the world so much that he got his hands and feet dirty, both literally and figuratively, with the soil and raw emotion of community living. Through Jesus, a new community—the church—is called into being, commissioned and anointed to share good news with a fractured and chaotic world.

Through Jesus, we have a message of hope to offer to the people around us. The church is increasingly facing the challenge of whether to engage with community or to retreat and disengage in order to prioritise piety and discipleship. The invitation from Hope Together (www.hopetogether.org.uk) is to use this year as a time to get to know our communities—to get our hands and feet dirty with the soil and raw emotion of community living—and to share good news, in action and conversation, with disillusioned and forgotten people.

Hope in our local communities, whether villages, towns, or cities, relies on our getting involved and loving the people whom God has brought to us. There is one guarantee: if we get it right, we and others in our locality will never be the same again.

The 'I am' sayings in John

John's Gospel has itself been called a 'seamless robe' (see John 19:23), for ideas and images weave back and forward across the Gospel, and we can easily move from an incident to theological reflection without noticing the join. However, readers have found structure in it. For example, John teasingly highlights the first two 'signs' that Jesus performed (John 2:11; 4:54), leaving us to speculate as to whether we should identify more. The 'I am' sayings are a similarly fine-sounding but somewhat ambiguous thread in John's Gospel. A quick internet search tells me that 'Jesus said "I am" on seven occasions'—which is simply untrue. In fact, the Gospel records him saying it 45 times, 25 of which are emphatic in Greek (*ego eimi*), but many of these don't seem particularly rich with meaning.

There are two reasons why the 'I am' sayings draw attention. First, the question 'Who is Jesus?' is an important one. What could be better than direct, clear, self-revelation from Jesus? Second, 'I am' has an important Old Testament pedigree. In Exodus 3:14, God reveals his name as YHWH (or Yahweh). The most plausible way of understanding this is that his name is 'I am' (presumably in the sense of 'the living one' or 'the ground of all being'). In addition, Isaiah 45 (especially verse 18) is a deeply monotheistic passage in which YHWH asserts his uniqueness. In the Hebrew, a slightly different word is used in Isaiah from that in Exodus, but the Greek translation uses 'I am' (*ego eimi*) as the key word in this assertion of divine uniqueness. Thus, there is good reason to see that, in the right context, 'I am' (*ego eimi*) links back to these passages of divine revelation in the Old Testament. Context is, of course, important. 'I am' is a normal Greek word: every time a Greek-speaking Jewish child said, 'I am hungry' or 'I am over here', they were obviously not deliberately echoing the divine name! As we read John together, you will have to make your own mind up about the significance of these occurrences.

Our week's study does not give us time to plumb the depths of John's Gospel. I have tried to select some key passages from the number of interesting occasions on which Jesus says, 'I am'. Quotations are taken from the New Revised Standard Version of the Bible.

1 The bread of life

John 6:25–35

This dialogue follows on from the feeding of the 5000. The people saw this sign (6:14) and eagerly pursued Jesus (vv. 22–24), but they have missed the point (v. 26). They have not understood about the loaves (to quote Mark 6:52).

The rest of the passage teases out this misunderstanding. The people think that 'heavenly bread' is simply normal food 'from heaven' (v. 31). They recognise that the feeding of the 5000 was, effectively, food from heaven, but they want something more dramatic or perhaps repeated, as the provision of the manna was (Exodus 16). Then they would recognise Jesus as a prophet like Moses (Deuteronomy 18:15). But Jesus challenges this idea: the manna was not really 'heavenly bread', merely 'bread from the sky, provided by God'. It perished (v. 27) because, whatever its source, it was normal food. What they really need is something far better than manna—the 'true bread from heaven' that 'gives life to the world' (vv. 32–33) and endures for eternal life (v. 27).

What does God require of us (v. 28, compare Micah 6:8)? It's a good question, but Jesus' answer is shocking. What God requires (potentially 'all' that God requires) is belief in the one he has sent (v. 29)—in other words, trust in himself. Coming to him and believing in him will result in true, permanent sustenance (v. 35) because he is the 'bread of life'.

It's easy for us to be like 'the people' in this passage. We look to God for provision ('bread from heaven'), but what we mean by that is provision for our ordinary needs: a successful meeting, catching the train, the bad weather holding off, the person becoming better. We look for manna, but Jesus' challenge is to raise our sights to the true bread of heaven, which brings something beyond physical sustenance. (Never being thirsty or hungry again must point to something beyond physical thirst and hunger: see, for example, Isaiah 55.) As we trust in him, our lives are sustained in a deeper and more significant way; then, with Paul we can say, 'I have learned to be content with whatever I have… I have learned the secret of being well-fed and of going hungry, of having plenty and of being in need. I can do all things through him who strengthens me' (Philippians 4:4, 11–13). When you pray 'Give us this day our daily bread', what are you asking for?

2 The light of the world

John 8:12; 9:1–7

Light appears several times in John's Gospel (see 1:4–8; 3:19–21; 5:35; 11:9–10; 12:35–36, 46) but in these two passages Jesus explicitly says, 'I am the light of the world.' The first is perhaps in the context of the feast of tabernacles (7:2), which was celebrated with great lights in the temple, but what follows from 8:12 focuses on Jesus' relationship to God. In John 9 we return to the idea of light, this time in connection with literal blindness.

Light is closely linked to the idea of life itself. Light was the first thing created by God (Genesis 1:3), and John's Gospel begins by closely connecting Jesus with both life and light, which cannot be destroyed by darkness (1:4–5). The psalmist declares that God is both light and salvation (Psalm 27:1). Light also reveals the path we should travel (Psalm 119:105: 'Your word is a lamp to my feet and a light to my path) and the truth about what people do (John 3:19–21).

Thus, if Jesus is the light of the world, he is the source of life (see, for example, 5:24–26) and of guidance (8:51; 14:23), and he brings judgment (5:22). John emphasises that Jesus' purpose is to bring salvation (3:16–17) and to be a blessing (12:35–36): the promised 'light to the nations' (Isaiah 49:6; see Luke 2:32) was for their good. But an inevitable consequence of light is that it reveals the truth: 'This is the judgment… people loved darkness rather than light because their deeds were evil' (John 3:19).

Thus we find a meaning behind the healing of the blind man (or, perhaps, his 'new creation', for he had never seen, and the use of mud is reminiscent of creation in Genesis 2:7). Eventually Jesus accuses the Pharisees of being 'blind' (9:39–41). This man's literal blindness had nothing to do with sin (vv. 2–3), but their wilful spiritual blindness does.

'Light of the world' captures in one image not only the life, goodness and joy that Jesus brings but also the inevitability of the judgment that he brings. As we walk through our days, we can reflect: would I welcome at this moment the warmth of Christ's light on me, or am I hesitant about what it would reveal?

3 The good shepherd

John 10:10–18

The 'good shepherd' would have had particular resonances in the predominantly rural areas where Jesus preached, as shepherds played an important part there. However, the image also has important Old Testament background, most notably in Ezekiel 34, where God accuses the 'shepherds' of his people of living well off the backs of the sheep but failing in their duty to care for them. In response, he says, he will come and shepherd them himself (34:11–16). Elsewhere Jesus uses the image of shepherd and sheep to speak of his mission (Luke 15:1–7).

The good shepherd focuses on the sheep's benefit: he is there for the sheep, not the sheep for the shepherd. Jesus' activity is aimed at giving us enjoyable, rich life (v. 10). This full life is amplified by the contrast with the thief (v. 10) and the 'hired hand' (v. 12). The thief is simply out to exploit the sheep, and even the hired hand puts his own interests before the sheep, who then suffer. Not so Jesus, the self-sacrificial good shepherd, who knows and cares for his sheep.

Three points of connect can be made with our lives. First, this passage speaks of the trust we can place in God. How often do we worry that following God's ways may bring good to others but may be worse for ourselves? But no, God gives good gifts to his children (Matthew 7:9–11): the good shepherd cares for his sheep. Second, what impression do we give others of what being a follower of Jesus means? Are we earnest but joyless, overly busy and suspicious of pleasure? This is at odds with Jesus' promise of 'abundant life' and hardly commends him to others. Third, there is a warning to those of us with leadership roles within families, jobs, communities and churches. Our shepherding should also be for the benefit of the sheep (see 1 Peter 5:1–4). Sometimes there might be the suspicion that a vicar wants the congregation to grow, or people to turn up at a speaker event, more so that he or she looks good than because it will benefit the people, or that our boss is interested in our success only because it will reflect well on him or her.

4 The resurrection and the life

John 11:17–27

Often enough, I find myself walking down a long aisle leading a coffin as I proclaim the words, '"I am the resurrection and the life," says the Lord. "Those who believe in me, even though they die, will live, and everyone who lives and believes in me will never die"' (taken from vv. 25–26). These words might seem like some sort of cruel joke (the loved ones are grieving precisely because someone has died) unless I believed them to be true. This is also the original context: Jesus is speaking with a grieving sister (here, as in Luke 10:38–42, Martha is more assertive than Mary), and here, perhaps, we see the Christian faith's greatest claim.

Martha expresses the right words, that God will do 'whatever you ask of him' (v. 22; compare Matthew 7:7–11; 21:22; John 15:7, 16). However, she doesn't think that this extends as far as seeing Lazarus coming back to life *now* (v. 24; see also vv. 39–40). Her 'whatever' really means 'whatever… given sensible expectations'—God will provide comfort, not action—but Jesus pushes her further. Life and death really are in his power. It is all about him: '*I* am the resurrection and the life.' God's plan to defeat suffering and death are focused on him (6:39–44). With Jesus, 'whatever' really does mean whatever; nothing is impossible for God.

Verses 25 and 26 expand on 'resurrection' and 'life' in turn. First, those who believe in him, although they die, will be brought back to life (see 5:21); second, those who believe in him can never be separated from true life (see 1:4; 5:24; 8:51). These concepts express the two sides of the Christian hope—that those who die 'sleep' until the resurrection (see, for example, 1 Thessalonians 4:13–17), but also that nothing, not even death, can separate us from our life in Christ (for example, Romans 8:38–39).

Alongside Martha, we are faced once more with the great claim of

Christianity: death was defeated by Jesus. Like Martha, we can tone this idea down to mean 'everything will be OK in the end', but there is nothing vague about Jesus' claim that he provides life that never ends, and brings the dead back to life.

5 The way, the truth and the life

John 14:1–11

This triplet links back to the previous saying, with its repetition of 'the life', but adds three important new concepts—'the way' (v. 4), the uniqueness of Jesus' role (v. 6) and the idea that Jesus reveals the Father (v. 9).

The first name given to Christianity seems to have been 'the Way' (see Acts 9:2; 18:25–26). This probably reflects Jesus' command to 'follow me' and his itinerant ministry (Matthew 8:19–23). His followers were called to leave things behind and journey with him (for example, Mark 1:16–20). It is also full of resonances of pilgrimage, or journeying to the promised land (see Hebrews 11:13–16). Jesus gives access to God (Hebrews 10:19–22).

Giving access to God is similar to revealing God (expressed in John 14 by 'knowing', 'showing' and 'seeing', vv. 7–9). Moses was told that nobody can see God (Exodus 33:18–23). This influenced later visionary literature, which contains both a longing to see God and a hesitation (for example, in Ezekiel 1). John's Gospel agrees that nobody can see God but, at the same time, claims that Jesus makes him known (see 1:18). Elsewhere we find the same idea expressed in different ways: Jesus is the 'image of the invisible God' (Colossians 1:15) and the 'reflection of God's glory and the exact imprint of God's very being' (Hebrews 1:3). If you want to know what God is like, look at Jesus.

The claim that 'no one comes to the Father except through me' (v. 6) has become important in thinking about other religions or belief systems. It seems to claim that Christianity is the only way to reach God. However, it doesn't quite say that. The unique and necessary role in giving access to God lies with Jesus, not Christianity. This verse is perfectly coherent with the view that other religions, philosophies or ways of life can point us towards God because they have something of Jesus in them—that the good person (perhaps a follower of another religion) is, unbeknown to them, being shown God by Jesus. Even so, this claim is unlikely to be welcomed by the followers of another religion. However, this is not really the focus of the passage. Its key thrust is about assurance: those who have seen Jesus (or know him) have, in fact, seen God (or know him), and they can be confident that they are travelling into God.

6 The vine

John 15:1–6

This final 'I am' saying differs from the others, for they were primarily statements about Jesus, not about us. We might see ourselves as the sheep being shepherded or those being led 'on the way', but a shepherd can exist without sheep. A vine without branches (tendrils/shoots/creepers), however, is at best a barren stick. Indeed, a picture of a pruned vine is shocking: it does look just like a lifeless stick, although in spring it rapidly shoots forth luscious green foliage, followed by fruit.

Thus, by stating that he is 'the vine', Jesus is proclaiming that we are integral to his identity. Without us, he seems to be lifeless, even pointless. This seems shocking: how can we be that important to God? But there is a deep truth here. Of course God existed before creation and is separate from creation, but the God of the Bible desires to create and to have relationship—walking in the garden with the humans he has made (Genesis 3:8). More profoundly, the reason why Jesus, the pre-existing eternal word, became flesh was to make God known (John 1:1, 14, 18) and bring salvation to us and the world (3:16; compare Romans 8:19–21). We belong with Jesus and he with us: he gives us life and we give him fruit.

In the Old Testament, the vine was an image of Israel (Jeremiah 2:21; Hosea 10:1). Thus we see here that Jesus effectively claims to be Israel itself, and it is those who 'abide' in him who are the true Israelites. Those who do not become lifeless and fruitless and, in the end, face judgment (8:31–47; Matthew 3:9–10). This reinforces the message of the 'I am' saying in John 14:6: 'No one comes to the Father except through me.'

No branch can have life, and it can certainly not produce fruit, except through Jesus.

To bear fruit, we need to be pruned (v. 2). This is a disturbing idea, yet most of us can see the point, not just in the horticultural context but also in our own lives. Often enough, some things have to stop, be brought to an end, even be 'cut away', to allow future growth. Yet it is difficult when we only see the point in retrospect, and it requires great trust in our Father, the vine grower (v. 1).

Guidelines

This week we have seen Jesus describe himself as the bread of life, the light of the world, the good shepherd, the resurrection and the life, the way, the truth and the life, and the vine. Each of these images has spoken to us about what Jesus does—the ways in which he sustains and aids us and the world, and leads us to and links us with God. But what does that say about who he is?

Three 'I am sayings' seem to point beyond Jesus' actions to his essence, and potentially echo the divine name ('I am'), as outlined in the introduction. Twice Jesus says 'I am' with the basic meaning of 'It's me'. The first occasion is when he walks across the lake to his disciples in the boat in the storm (6:20) and tells them, 'Don't be afraid.' The miraculous context of mastery over the stormy waters certainly connects with Old Testament passages describing God himself (see, for example, Job 38:8–11; Psalms 89:9; 107:23–32). The second is in Gethsemane (18:6), when his words 'I am (he)' causes the soldiers to 'step back and fall to the ground'—an odd reaction, except that fear and falling to the ground are standard responses to a divine revelation. The other occasion is in John 8:58, when, at the climax of a dialogue about who are the true descendants of Abraham and about whether or not he has seen Abraham, Jesus proclaims, 'Before Abraham was, I am.' On the face of it, this is a claim to some sort of existence prior to being born from Mary. In response, people attempt to stone him—the usual response to blasphemy.

These 'I am' sayings, then, speak to us of Jesus' function (what he does and how he acts) but they also point beyond that to who he truly is—God made flesh. We too have many functions and roles: for example, I am a father, a vicar, a son, a husband, a neighbour and a friend. How do these functions connect with a deeper sense of who I am? We might think of our churches: how do the things that the church does, and how it does them, point beyond to God himself? Or we might return to pondering the works of God themselves, praying that God would open our eyes so that, through the things around us and the people we meet, we see him, the 'I am', who creates, sustains and saves all of creation.

Matthew 7—10

If you have been following the previous Gospel studies in *Guidelines*, you should have a clear picture of what was important to Jesus and what a messianic lifestyle is like. This is a demanding way. To follow Jesus is to share in the 'upside-down kingdom', since it involves a reversal of the assumptions and values we take for granted.

At the beginning of the Sermon on the Mount (Matthew 5), we noted several ways of interpreting it. One way argues that the Sermon pitches God's moral demands so far beyond us that we are unable to implement them. It is given to expose our moral inability and to drive us to Christ as the only one who is qualified to save us. It certainly does this, although we should remember that the Sermon does not say, 'Accomplish all this and you will be saved'. Rather, as with the Old Testament law, it says, 'Now that you have been saved by grace through faith, this is the pattern of life you are empowered to live.'

A second interpretation understands the Sermon to be cultivating within us the individual habits and dispositions that will make us into good and virtuous people. There is much to challenge us here, provided we understand that this is more than a moralistic, ethical change that we have to produce by our unaided efforts. We cannot live this life unless we are previously rooted in the life and fellowship of the Messiah. Empowered and inspired by his Spirit, we can do surprisingly more than we imagine.

Moreover, following a third interpretation, the Sermon is not meant to be lived by isolated and unsupported individuals. It describes the quality of life, the alternative lifestyle, of a 'contrast society' that looks to Jesus as its inspiration, with him dwelling in its midst (Matthew 18:20). This is nothing less than a new and revolutionary movement embodying all the virtues and qualities that the Sermon outlines. Far from being unattainable, this point of view affirms, everything described here can, with God's and each other's help, become a visible, embodied reality in the community of Jesus' followers. We should put it into practice and keep each other up to the mark in following the Way that Christ has pioneered for us.

Quotations are taken from the New Revised Standard Version unless stated otherwise.

1 Guidance and encouragement

Matthew 7:1–11

It is important to understand the difference between 'judging' as standing in judgment over others and 'judging' in the sense of discerning between truth and error. In the latter sense, the apostle Paul indicates that 'those who are spiritual discern all things' (1 Corinthians 2:15). We have to exercise spiritual and ethical judgment and do so constantly, especially if we are in positions of leadership. This is different from standing in judgment on others, which suggests that we are superior to them and are without personal fault. Jesus points out that we frequently find faults in others while remaining blind to our own, which may be much greater.

The 'speck' and the 'log' (vv. 3–5) are hyperbole and an example of Jesus' humour. The blame culture is best avoided. Responsible discernment is to be encouraged. An example of responsible judgment might be seen in Jesus' words about throwing pearls before swine (v. 6). There is no point in offering highly valued truths to people who show no sign of being able to receive them and who would trample on them if offered. There are enough responsive people in the world not to waste time on those who (at least at this point) are not interested. In 10:14 Jesus will instruct his disciples to 'shake off the dust from your feet' when they find no response.

After giving this guidance, Jesus offers huge encouragement to those who are seeking God or are engaged in prayer: God will respond to asking, searching and knocking on the door (vv. 7–8). Here is a word for all who are hungry for God but have not yet found him or are praying earnestly. If you continue to seek, you will find. The fact that there are two threefold repetitions here adds double emphasis to this promise. Most helpful of all is Jesus' typical argument from the lesser to the greater in verse 11 (a common Jewish way of arguing): if we who are 'evil' care for our children and want to give them only good things, how much more will God, who is infinitely kind and good, give good and wholesome things to us. This implies that if we ask for harmful things, God will not grant them.

2 Authenticity

Matthew 7:12–23

This section contains the 'golden rule' ('Do to others as you would have them do to you', v. 12), which is echoed in many different religions and philosophies. For moral guidance we will be close to the mark if we foster empathy and altruism and treat other people as we would like them to treat us. This may not answer every dilemma but it will take care of most. Authentic, godly living begins with this straightforward rule.

However, although it is simply stated, it is not always easy to do. That is why Jesus talks about the narrow gate and the hard road and contrasts them with the broad road, which is easy to follow but leads to destruction (vv. 13–14). Following the crowd is not a good rule for moral action. 'Everybody else does it' is not a valid argument. Those who seek the good life will often find themselves in the minority. Moreover, there is an indication here about how we enter the kingdom. A narrow gate can be passed through by only one person at a time. We do not enter the kingdom on somebody else's ticket but on our own account, through our own decision and response to Christ. Although we believe in the messianic community, there is a kind of individualism involved in following Jesus and being part of that community. We have to take up our cross and follow him, to be born again to see the kingdom of God.

The rest of this section underlines the point: we are known by our fruits (vv. 16–20). We can discern a true prophet from a false one by their actions. When a person's heart has been transformed, then they can produce that which is good. It is not enough only to hear what a person says: Jesus distinguishes not between salvation by works and salvation by faith but between what we claim and what we are (v. 21). There are those who say the right thing and even, apparently, do acts of power, but in reality they are not of God. Do not be deceived. This is a challenge to us: 'Examine yourselves to see whether you are living in the faith. Test yourselves' (2 Corinthians 13:5). The proof that we are genuine, that we really have been inwardly transformed by grace through faith, is that we do 'the will of my Father in heaven' (Matthew 7:21).

3 The authority of Jesus

Authentic followers of Jesus put the teaching of their Messiah into practice. They are not simply hearers of what he said but active practitioners of the lifestyle he demonstrated. Jesus did not so much practise what he preached as preach what he practised. So it should be with us. Our witness to God springs from what we live, not simply from what we hear. We hear the words of Jesus and act on them. In this way we lay solid foundations. When the storms of doubt, opposition or tribulation come and put us to the test, we are able to stand firm because the way of Jesus is like a rock on which we build (v. 25).

In fact, the idea of 'hearing' in scripture means much more than casually listening. We hear, then we absorb what we hear until it becomes part of us, and then we live out the teaching because it is embedded within us. We take the authority of Jesus seriously. In Jesus' day, and even today in Judaism, it was common for rabbis to argue with reference to what other rabbis before them had taught. Jesus took the Hebrew scriptures as his authority but it was not his practice to refer to the rabbinic traditions. He did not appeal to precedent but dared to teach on his own authority. We have already seen this repeatedly in Matthew 5: 'You have heard it said… but I say to you.' The appeal to his own authority to interpret and apply the law of Israel marks Jesus out and says something about how he regarded himself.

The impact of this practice upon his hearers was startling (vv. 28–29). It was not only that it was unusual but that it was, potentially, pretentious. Those who are not believers in Jesus must still feel the same way. Was he mad or bad, possessed of visions of grandeur or a false prophet? This is a dilemma that has often been posed. Were it not that he was truly sent from God, truly the Messiah and the Son of God, we would have to conclude that he was under a mighty illusion. For those, however, who say to Jesus, 'Lord, Lord', and truly mean it, the conclusion is otherwise. He had the right to say what he said because he was the person he claimed to be.

4 Healing ministry

Matthew 8:1–17

From the words of the Sermon on the Mount, we now follow Jesus as he engages in a widespread ministry of healing and deliverance. Jesus was both a healer and an exorcist. He had authority to teach but also to exercise spiritual power. This was one consequence of his reception of the Spirit at his baptism, through which he was installed publicly as the Messiah.

In today's reading we learn of the cleansing of a leper (a word used in those days to indicate a sufferer from a range of chronic skin diseases), of the servant of a centurion (a senior Roman officer who was probably retired and living in Capernaum, Jesus' adopted home), and of Peter's mother-in-law. We would like to know more about all these people. The very fact that Peter had a mother-in-law is intriguing: we know very few domestic details about the disciples or about Jesus himself.

'Leprosy' was a particularly feared ailment and lepers were excluded from mainstream society. Elisha had authenticated his prophetic status by cleansing Naaman the leper (2 Kings 5:8). Jesus tells the man to go to the priest so that, in accordance with Jewish law, the priest might certify his recovery (v. 4). This shows an important aspect of Jesus' healing ministry: the excluded sick were both made well and re-included in the community, particularly the worshipping community.

The healing of the centurion's servant and the display of the centurion's understanding and faith is the occasion for a visionary insight in verses 11–12, with profound significance for Jesus and the church. Jesus sees believing Gentiles gathering for the feast of the age to come while some in Israel are excluded from it (presumably because of their lack of faith). By contrast, Jews believed that all Israel would have a share in 'the age to come'.

This section ends with a glorious picture of the needy being brought to Jesus at evening time. The demonised were liberated by a mere word from Jesus' lips and the sick were cured. On two occasions in this reading, Jesus brings healing by a touch, and this suggests both the compassionate gentleness of the way he dealt with the vulnerable and the mediation of healing from Jesus himself into their bodies. Jesus was truly a healing agent, able to bring life and wholeness to the afflicted.

5 Momentum builds

Matthew 8:18–22

As we progress through chapter 8, we can feel the excitement and momentum building. Wherever Jesus goes, the level of excitement and expectation increases. Signs and wonders abound and people are amazed. The authority of Jesus is on full display. These are the years of Jesus' popularity, and he is mobbed. The crowds press upon him so hard that he has to find ways of escaping them (v. 18).

It will not always be so. Enthusiasts declare their desire to follow him but Jesus does not make it easy for them. Rather, he seems to put people off (vv. 20–22). Contrast this with our own times, when we are tempted to set the threshold for entry to the kingdom at a minimal level. To the scribe who wishes to follow him wherever he goes, Jesus speaks of his itinerant and unsettled existence. To the disciple who would like to follow him but not quite yet (burying one's father was an important filial duty and his father might not be dead yet), Jesus' words are also a rebuke. Cutting through their superficial enthusiasm, Jesus faces them with the true cost of being a disciple. To have disciples in the good times is one thing, but whether they will last the course is another (see John 6:66–71). Jesus is testing his disciples to gauge the quality of their commitment.

Here also we are introduced to a further title of Jesus. In Matthew 4, his identity as the Son of God is tested (4:3, 6). Here, Jesus identifies himself as the Son of Man (v. 20). Debate abounds as to what this means. For some, it is simply a roundabout way of saying 'I'. For others, it is a title going back to the visions of the book of Daniel, where 'one like a son of man' was given dominion and glory and a kingdom 'that shall not be destroyed' (7:13–14, RSV). If the latter is the case, then Jesus is claiming a significant title for himself that marks him out as God's chosen agent for the fulfilment of all things. The title crops up frequently in the Gospels and it seems unlikely that it is simply a way of referring to himself as a human being or of saying 'I'.

6 Mystery and attestation

Matthew 8:23—9:1

Despite the emerging clues that the reader is supposed to pick up, it is clear that not even his closest disciples understood as yet exactly who Jesus was. The Gospels very rarely portray the disciples in a complimentary light, instead pointing out their slowness and the frustration of Jesus with them, as here in verse 26. This should be a sign of the reliability of the Gospels: usually we whitewash our heroes, but not so here.

When, with a command, Jesus calms a frightening storm on Lake Galilee, he provokes questions about who he must be to be able to do this (v. 27). The disciples asked Jesus to save them and he did. Matthew portrays Jesus as being like God, Lord over nature, exercising divine authority over creation, being the Saviour and protector of those who call on him.

Having safely crossed the lake, Jesus is no longer in Jewish territory. He is on alien soil where herds of pigs are found, quite unlike Israel, where pigs were unclean. For the locals he represents a frightening figure, probably because of his spiritual authority, which overawes them, and the threat to the local economy that they see in him (with reason). This is evident in the astonishing deliverance of the demoniacs who inhabited the tombs. It must surely be the same incident as the deliverance of Legion described in Mark 5:1–20, where the details are fuller but the pigs are dealt with in the same way. Why Matthew has two demoniacs is a mystery. Perhaps he knows something that Mark and we do not, or perhaps he is telescoping this incident with another to save space (he doubles up in other places: see 9:27–31 and 20:29–34).

The deliverance of the demoniacs is more important in Jesus' eyes than the fate of the swine. Today we would assume that the men were mentally ill, but we would be ill-advised to exclude the category of 'the demonic'. Not everything that happens to human beings can be explained in terms of medical categories. Jesus' authority is seen in the way he immediately deals with the demons that are infesting them. Strikingly, whereas the disciples are still questioning who Jesus must be, the demons have no doubts whatsoever (v. 29). His presence is a torment to them. This is the Son of God and their time has come. Jesus casts them out with a word (v. 32). As the tension mounts, so does the mystery of who Jesus is.

Guidelines

We imagine we would have welcomed Jesus, had we been there. After reading this chapter, how would you have responded to him? How do you do so now?

Those for whom Jesus is very much a friend might find it hard to imagine him as a frightening figure: the people in this region begged Jesus to go away, they were so afraid of him (and perhaps of the potential threat he posed to the local economy). But the 'fear of the Lord' is surely appropriate when we take seriously the holiness of God and the threat that his presence poses to our sins and shortcomings. Do we underestimate the extent to which Jesus turns our lives upside down? Do we also underestimate his power to set us free? Are there areas of your life where you are bound and need to be liberated?

Reflect on the titles 'Son of God' and 'Son of Man'. How do they relate to each other?

28 July–3 August

1 Healing and forgiveness

Matthew 9:2–13

Jesus is back in Capernaum, his home town. Going by boat was by far the swiftest and safest way to travel. The healing ministry continues without a pause as friends bring a paralysed man to be healed. Although it is Jesus whose power heals, it is clear in this passage that faith plays an important role. We can think of faith as receptivity to the power of God, mingled with trust. Where this is present, Jesus can give and we can receive.

Jesus forgives the man's sin (v. 2). It is not clear here whether the paralysis is considered to be a consequence of sin or whether Jesus simply forgives his sins for good measure. In either case, to know you are forgiven is conducive to good health. Some scribes/theologians who are there regard this action as blasphemous. Strictly, for them, blasphemy meant profaning God's name, which Jesus did not nor ever would do. However, by associating himself so closely with God and using God's authority to forgive, Jesus may, in their view, have been going too far.

In verse 6 we notice the title Son of Man once more, and the awe and amazement resulting in glory to God after the healing. If Jesus gave offence because he associated himself with God, he also gave offence through the human company he kept. Tax collectors like Matthew (who may or may not have been the author of the Gospel) were charged with collecting local customs duties. There was little regulation and they could easily add a premium for themselves. They were not popular, yet Jesus called Matthew (v. 9). Jesus ate with tax collectors and sinners, people who were regarded as disruptive of community welfare. Although this attracted criticism from respectable Pharisees, Jesus saw his actions as expressions of divine mercy. Jesus does not deny that the Pharisees are righteous but he does understand that his mission is to those who are not (v. 13). He has come to call them into the kingdom and into fellowship with God. If we ever forget this, we are forgetting something of great importance to God. If we are to be like God, showing friendship and hospitality to 'sinners' is part of our task.

2 Compassionate presence

Matthew 9:14–38

This section ends with a very fine summary of the ministry of Jesus as an itinerant preacher and teacher and as a compassionate and loving healer of the sick. All of these ministries belong together. Jesus preached good news to the people in the open air, gave group teaching in the synagogues (which were secular as well as religious meeting places) and made it all highly personal as he cured the sick.

Once more we see the impact of Jesus' touch: a woman with a long-standing haemorrhage had only to touch the fringes (*tzitzit*—customary for Jewish men to wear) of his cloak in the middle of the crowd to be made well. Jesus apparently felt her touch and recognised the woman's faith. Then he took the hand of a little girl being mourned as dead and restored her to life. He touched the eyes of two blind men and their sight was restored. Jesus' physical and spiritual presence among the people brought God's word and God's power to them.

For many, the work he did bore no comparison to anything that had ever happened before in Israel. They welcomed him as the Son of David (v. 27) and the Son of Man (9:6). Yet even a great work of God is susceptible to distorted interpretations. Perhaps some modern interpreters would find purely psychosomatic interpretations of Jesus' undoubtedly powerful impact. They might point to other known wonder-workers in different religions and minimise Jesus by categorising and relativising him. He was just a shaman, they might say. In his own day, his opponents did not deny Jesus' power but attributed it to demons. Jesus was therefore, in their eyes, a fake, a deceiver of the people, endowed with supra-normal powers by the 'ruler of the demons' (v. 34).

We may counter this by saying that although there are indeed counterfeit acts of power (look back to 7:22), the love and compassion that Jesus showed are not something within the power of demons to produce. Finally, the test of Jesus' authenticity and right to be acknowledged is not the awesome nature of his works but the mercy and compassion that lie behind them. As Jesus looked at the crowds, 'he had compassion for them' (v. 36). They were like sheep in need of a shepherd like Jesus who would take them to his heart.

3 Labourers for the harvest

Matthew 10:1–15

Even as Jesus asked his hearers to pray to God to raise up new workers, he was already answering his own prayer. Jesus needed to reproduce his own ministry in and through his disciples. This chapter begins with the names of those who were included in the close circle around him. Jesus chose twelve because this was the number of the patriarchs and the tribes of Israel. Within Israel, Jesus was intent on creating a renewal movement to revitalise the whole nation.

We have already met some of these disciples, but the list of names introduces Judas, who was to betray him. In gathering these men around him, Jesus was laying the foundations of the community that would become the church and, in time, carry forward his work. Some form of recognised and appointed leadership has always been a necessity for the church, right from the start. Jesus endowed these apostles (which means 'sent ones') with spiritual authority akin to his own and gave them clear instructions as to how to conduct themselves.

Would curing the sick, raising the dead, cleansing lepers, and casting out demons (v. 8) be an appropriate job description for ministers today? The first leaders of the church were not religious functionaries but powerful emissaries with spiritual authority. Their first priority was to restore the lost sheep of Israel, to continue and extend the works of Jesus and to do it in a way that had complete integrity. In this holy mission, they were to rely on God to provide and connect with those who were 'worthy' (vv. 11, 13)—that is, those whose hearts were open to receive them and their message. Where there was no ready welcome, they were to move on, shaking the dust from their feet. The task was urgent and time could not be wasted.

Sodom and Gomorrah were destroyed for lack of charity and hospitality and other forms of immorality (Genesis 19; Ezekiel 16:49–50). God will deal in his own way with those who resist the message.

4 Consequences

Matthew 10:16–25

It should not surprise us that the way people responded to Jesus was repeated in the way they responded to his representatives (v. 25). Disciples, says Jesus, are not above their Master. Jesus was welcomed by some and rejected by some others. By the time Matthew wrote his Gospel, Christians had multiplied across the Mediterranean world and had received a welcome in many places, but they were already beginning to feel the full force of rejection and persecution. Remembering these words of Jesus would have been particularly poignant at such times, as it still is today.

Some of the opposition came from the synagogues (v. 17). Although it is absolutely right to affirm the kinship of Christians and Jews and to recognise the 'Nazarenes' as a movement emerging from Judaism, the words of Jesus here indicate that exclusion from synagogues was one form of rejection that his disciples would encounter. This was particularly painful for the church, since the Jews had a special protected status within the Roman empire, a kind of 'opt-out' from the religious pluralism that Rome fostered. Once the Christians had been thrust out from under the umbrella of Judaism, they were vulnerable to outright persecution. We may celebrate the fact that there are now many Jews who believe in Jesus and that, in general, Christians and Jews are learning to appreciate what they have in common, even though they may still differ about Jesus as Messiah.

More persecution would come from the pagan powers that governed Rome. Because of their loyalty to Jesus and the insistence that he alone (and not Caesar) was Lord, Christians were a target for scapegoating and discrimination. The disciples would not be spared these things, but they would be given resources in the midst of them. God would help them bear their testimony along the way through the Spirit. It is ironic that Jesus, who came to bring peace, would actually be the trigger for division, not by his own choice but by reason of the varying responses to him. Jesus is a threat to sinful ways. In the same way, the messianic community, though a community of peace, causes a polarisation of opinions about it. It is essential that we remain steadfastly a community of peacemakers (Matthew 5:9–11), even though others do not comprehend or value the light that shines forth.

5 More consequences

Matthew 10:32–39

We skip forward a few verses (just for today) to revisit the inevitable truth that Jesus' own teaching and the church's preaching about him are bound to cause division. Jesus makes the stark statement that he has come to bring 'not… peace, but a sword' (v. 34). Sometimes in the Bible generally and in the teaching of Jesus in particular, consequences are portrayed as intentions. Further examples can be found in Isaiah 6:9–10 and Matthew 13:13–15. This is an idiomatic way of speaking, which communicates the fact that even though it is not God's will or intention for people to reject the message, when they do so it comes as no surprise. God knows and foresees that they will reject it and yet he persists in pursuing the divine purpose.

There is therefore a bitter irony that, despite the purpose of God that all should be embraced, some will refuse. God knows that the gospel will divide opinion and response, yet it has to be this way in order that the hearers of the message may be precipitated into a decision. Those who acknowledge Christ will be acknowledged by the Father; those who deny him will be denied (v. 32). If the message of Jesus (and the message of John the Baptist before him) was that people should repent, for the kingdom was near (3:2; 4:17), then a decision was required—and that decision had to be a personal one.

We see here, once more, a kind of individualism to the gospel that requires us to decide on our own account, even if that puts us at odds with members of our own family (vv. 35–36). It is a decision that supersedes family loyalties. The Christian faith is not 'family-friendly' at this point, since neither the family nor the nation ranks higher than Christ. We must love our families but we must love God more. In fact, we should love God more than our very lives. If, through self-assertion and self-centredness, we seek to find life, we shall in fact lose it. Ironically, paradoxically, those who yield up their lives for Christ's sake will actually find life.

6 Reassurance

Matthew 10:26–31, 40–42

As we look at the remaining verses of Matthew 10, we ask the question, is following Jesus worthwhile? If we are to risk rejection, betrayal and persecution, taking up the cross and living the life of self-denial for Christ's sake, what is the guarantee that the course we have decided to take is better and more worthy than the one from which we have turned? The only guarantee is the promise of the Lord himself.

In these verses, which surround the warnings of division, Jesus speaks tender words about divine vindication. In the coming judgment, everything will become clear and will be seen for what it is (v. 26). Judgment is not (primarily) about God handing out punishment but about God setting things right, letting everything be seen in true perspective. The only one to fear is God's own self. The one who can 'destroy both soul and body in Gehenna' is not Satan (satirised by Jesus in verse 25 as Beelzebul, or 'Lord of the flies') but God. God values us, knows us and cares for us, and will not forsake us or deny us (vv. 30–31).

In sending out the apostles and the whole church, including ourselves, God will be with us. Christ treats us as his own representatives just as he is the one who represents God to us. Where we are welcomed by others, Christ and the Father are welcomed (v. 40). This gives Christians, and their commissioned ministers in particular, an astonishing status: we are as Christ to people. God is not careless about the way we are received, since this is a measure of how God's Son is being received. Those who welcome and receive us will be rewarded accordingly (vv. 41–42). Those who bless us will be blessed, and the outcome of our risky and costly service of God is not in doubt. God is to be trusted; God's providential care is to be relied upon (v. 30); God's final triumph over all the forces that oppose is certain. So we are to think highly of ourselves as we are in Christ. We are not to be arrogant—we are Christ's 'little ones' (v. 42)—but we are to think highly of the calling with which we are called and the mission for which we are commissioned.

Guidelines

Having to make decisions that will determine the shape of our lives for ever after is bound to provoke anxiety, especially when we are not sure what that future will hold. Much in our lives is determined and shaped by factors we cannot control. We cannot choose when and where we are born, or even whether we are born at all. We do not select our sex, our genetic inheritance, our racial and ethnic identity, the quality of our brain cells, our talents or our IQ. These things are given to us. Life deals us a hand—but a hand has to be played, so, although we are shaped and constrained and determined by many factors, we are not automata or machines. We are more than our genes. Our decisions determine the ways we will build upon what we have been given, and certain decisions are life-defining: for example, the decision to marry a particular person irrevocably pushes us in a certain direction (we hope, for good).

The Christ who encounters us in the passages we have studied is one who calls us to a decision about our fundamental loyalties. Will we make him the supreme reference point? Will we welcome him? Will we confess him to be the Messiah? The decision to do so is all-defining. It will affect our family relationships and our attitude to the wealth we acquire or inherit. It will give content to our future hopes. It will bring us into a place of prayer. It will have consequences for the circles in which we choose to move, especially whether we are part of a Christian community. It will shape the way we spend our time, which career we follow or which options we choose in following that career. Even more, if we join Christ in his mission, as he invites us to, risk and effort are necessary as we seek (in his name and strength) to do the kinds of work he himself did with the same goal in mind—that of the coming kingdom.

All that we have studied in the past fortnight causes us to conclude that following Jesus is not an easy ride, but nor is it without reward or profit, and not all of the reward is in 'the age to come'. Following Christ gives us a framework in which to understand the purpose of our lives. In fellowship with God's promised presence, there is great joy. Being part of the community of his followers enriches our relationships. To be defined by and in Christ is a rich treasure, greatly to be desired.

FURTHER READING

Leon Morris, *The Gospel According to Matthew*, Eerdmans, 1992.

John R.K. Stott, *Christian Counter-culture: The message of the Sermon on the Mount*, IVP, 1978.

Tom Wright, *Matthew for Everyone, Part 1: Chapters 1—15*, SPCK, 2002.

War and peace (I)

Through the centuries, Christians have wrestled with issues of war and peace. To some it seems obvious that followers of Jesus should not employ lethal violence. To many more, the realities of a violent world and glaring injustices seem to necessitate war, at least as a last resort. For others still, war has taken on the lustre of a crusade against evil.

The early churches were predominantly committed to non-participation in all forms of lethal violence. Church leaders taught it and imposed church discipline on those who contravened this teaching. Soldiers who converted were expected to leave the army or serve in non-combatant roles.

However, as the church grew and assumed increasing social responsibility—especially after the 'Christendom shift', when the emperor decided that Christianity should become the imperial religion—new ways of thinking developed. While war was never the first option, most now taught that in certain well-defined circumstances it was justifiable. These circumstances were based on stringent criteria, known as the 'just war' doctrine.

Not everyone was persuaded. Individuals, communities and movements over the next several centuries refused to 'make peace with war' and recovered the approach of the early Christians. Under no circumstances, they argued, should followers of Jesus participate in or support warfare. The search for justice must be pursued in other ways. The notes this week explore biblical passages that resonate with Christians in the 'peace church' tradition. This minority stance is gaining support as people inside and outside the churches recognise the repeated failure of 'redemptive violence' to establish justice and peace.

Biblical quotations are taken from the New International Version.

4–10 August

1 Swords into ploughshares

Isaiah 2:1–5

This is the first of four evocative visions of the mountain of God in Isaiah. The others are in chapters 11, 25 and 65. The prophet anticipates the time when all nations will convene at this mountain, summoned by God to learn to live in peace. Later visions promise long and fruitful lives, a wonderful banquet, creation in harmony, and sorrow and pain banished, culminating in new heavens and a new earth. This first vision invites us to imagine armaments converted into farming tools.

The word that describes this glorious vision is *shalom*. Often translated 'peace', it also implies prosperity, justice, wholeness, integration, community, joy, liberation, well-being, salvation and more—everything you could wish for those you love. *Shalom* envisages peace between God and humanity, disintegrated personalities healed, communities flourishing, enemies reconciled, weapons of war transformed into agricultural implements, injustice and oppression removed, creation liberated from bondage, and the abolition of sickness and death.

Shalom is the Old Testament equivalent of what the New Testament means by the kingdom of God. *Shalom* is the dream of God, the goal of creation, the hope of universal restoration. Peace is at the heart of the gospel because God's multi-directional and multi-dimensional mission is to bring *shalom* to the whole cosmos.

This vision is one of the most frequently quoted texts in early church writings. Justin, a teacher martyred in Rome in the second century, wrote:

We… delighted in war, in the slaughter of one another, and in every other kind of iniquity; [but we] have in every part of the world converted our weapons of war into implements of peace— our swords into ploughshares, our spears into farmers' tools—and we cultivate piety, justice, brotherly charity, faith and hope, which we derive from the Father through the crucified Saviour.

Non-violence must have seemed an impractical strategy in the face of Rome's mighty armies, but it was this vision of *shalom* that empowered the church to spread across the Roman empire, to outlast it and outnarrate it. How tragic, then, that as the empire embraced the gospel, the church forgot this glorious vision.

2 The Prince of Peace

If God's mission is to bring *shalom* to all creation, how will this happen? There is little evidence of peace advancing across the globe. Isaiah focuses our hope on a light in the darkness, a child to whom he ascribes extraordinary titles, one of which is 'Prince of Peace'. A new kind of ruler is coming, with a new kind of kingdom, whose reign will be characterised by justice and peace.

For centuries this remarkable prophecy went unfulfilled but not forgotten. Then John the Baptist's father proclaimed that a new dawn was breaking, light was shining in the darkness, and his baby son would 'guide our feet into the path of peace' (Luke 1:79). Then, as another child was born, an angelic choir sang, 'Glory to God in the highest heaven, and on earth peace to those on whom his favour rests' (Luke 2:14). Peace is the hope and promise of Advent.

Not that the birth and subsequent life, death and resurrection of Jesus abolished strife, violence and hatred. Indeed, as Simeon warned Jesus' mother, 'This child is destined to cause the falling and rising of many in Israel, and to be a sign that will be spoken against, so that the thoughts of many hearts will be revealed. And a sword will pierce your own soul too' (Luke 2:34–35).

Jesus' life, from Herod's desperate attempt to destroy him as an infant to his crucifixion, was marked by violence and the threat of violence. His teaching was divisive in a fractured society whose only experience of peace was 'Pax Romana'— the enforced subservience of subject populations that is the antithesis to the vision of *shalom*.

Isaiah 9, however, foretold the birth of one who would inaugurate a peaceful kingdom. The soldiers' boots and bloody uniforms will be destroyed, Isaiah writes (v. 6), and the seemingly endless cycle of violence and retaliation that disfigures human history will end. The Prince of Peace invites us to enter his kingdom, embrace its values and priorities, reject the myth of 'redemptive violence' and align ourselves with the coming *shalom* that God will establish.

3 Seek the peace of the city

Jeremiah 29:1–7

Shalom may be, as I have described it, 'everything you could wish for those you love', but what about your enemies? The Israelite exiles in Babylon were disorientated, grief-stricken and resentful. To enter into their emotions, read Psalm 137, one of the most violent and vindictive biblical texts. Far from seeking *shalom* for their captors, they wanted revenge, but Jeremiah urges them to see God's hand in their captivity and respond differently.

Not only should they abandon their nostalgia for Jerusalem and ignore the dreams of false prophets, not only must they settle down and learn to live in Babylon, resisting the temptation to despair, but also they are to 'seek the peace and prosperity of the city'. They are to pray for this enemy city to experience *shalom*. It is difficult to imagine a greater contrast to the spirit of Psalm 137.

Many scholars today draw parallels between the experience of the Israelites in Babylon and the situation of Christians in Western societies as Christendom fades. In our post-Christendom culture, we no longer feel at home. We have diminishing resources with which to grapple with the opportunities and challenges of this new mission context, and we need to think afresh about how the gospel engages with our culture.

In this unsettling environment, we can easily label others as 'the enemy'—secularists who scorn our faith, members of other faith communities who are gaining ground as we lose ground, the media that misrepresent us, and others. Christians complain about discrimination and some (inappropriately) label it 'persecution'. We are pilgrims in a world we no longer control, a minority with memories of being a majority, struggling to adjust. It is easy to become resentful and look for someone to blame.

Perhaps Jeremiah's message applies to us, too. What would it mean for us to seek *shalom* for our society? How might we love those whom we are tempted to regard as our enemies? Jeremiah tells the exiles that their *shalom* is dependent on Babylon's experiencing *shalom*. What might this mean for us in post-Christendom?

4 Love your enemies

Powerful as these Old Testament passages are, it is to the teaching of Jesus that the 'peace church' tradition looks as the foundation for its commitment to non-violence, and this section of the Sermon on the Mount is crucial. As followers of Jesus, we are not only to love God and our neighbours. We are also to love our enemies.

Responding to the question 'Who is my neighbour?' (Luke 10:29), Jesus eroded the distinction between neighbour and enemy in the parable of the good Samaritan. In Matthew 5, Jesus indicates that loving those who love us is normal, but enemy-loving reflects God's character.

What does enemy-loving mean, though? Staying silent and passive in the face of injustice? That hardly squares with the life of Jesus reported in the Gospels. It is possible to interpret the examples that Jesus gives—turning the other cheek, going the second mile, surrendering your cloak and tunic—as passive responses to injustice, but the cultural context suggests something more provocative. These are non-violent and gracious forms of resistance, challenging dehumanising practices with surprising actions.

There is an unhelpful similarity between the words 'pacifism' and 'passivism'. Jesus was not passive in his engagement with the poor and the powerful, Gentiles and religious leaders. His words and actions were frequently confrontational. Enemy-loving, it seems, requires courage, creativity and persistence. A friend has coined the term 'shalom activism' to capture the dynamism of this approach.

Through the centuries, various strategies have been employed to escape the challenge of this passage—for example, regarding it as a 'counsel of perfection', confining it to priests and monks, relegating it to God's future kingdom, applying it only to the personal sphere and not the public, or suggesting that it refers only to intentions (so you can kill your enemies lovingly!).

There have been arguments about how this passage relates to Old Testament texts in which God apparently approves of warfare and New Testament texts that could be interpreted as authenticating violence—but maybe Jesus meant what he said. Maybe he was standing in the prophetic tradition and urging his disciples to live towards the vision of shalom.

5 The good news of peace

Acts 10:25–48

This is an extraordinary incident. Luke recognises its significance and tells the story at length. He then records Peter's account to the Jerusalem church and their struggle to accept this unexpected and, at first, unwelcome development (Acts 11:1–18). The gospel, they reluctantly concluded, was not only for Jews (and maybe Samaritans) but also for Gentiles. This would change everything. All kinds of theological and cultural issues would have to be addressed. Peter's visit to Cornelius set in motion a train of conversations and events that continues today as we explore ways in which the gospel has an impact on diverse cultures.

We should not underestimate how difficult Peter found this visit to Cornelius. It required a vision from heaven to persuade him to go. He was profoundly uneasy. He was in the home of his enemy. Cornelius was a Roman centurion, an officer in the army that occupied Peter's homeland and was imposing order on a subjugated people. What might be a modern equivalent? Perhaps an Iraqi evangelist having tea in the Pentagon during the invasion of Iraq.

There were further challenges. As Peter listened to Cornelius explaining why he had summoned him, he heard about his enemy's prayer life, his care for the poor and the message he had received from an angel. Startled, Peter began his evangelistic talk by acknowledging that his own understanding of God's mission had expanded: 'I now realise…' (v. 34). Authentic evangelism involves two-way learning as we discover that God is ahead of us and beckoning us into new understandings. Cornelius is converted, but so is Peter—to a fresh revelation of God's grace.

There are many ways of presenting the gospel and telling the story of Jesus, but, in the house of his enemy, Peter focused on 'the good news of peace' (v. 36). After all, *shalom* was breaking out all around him as he explained what God had done through Jesus and invited a Roman centurion to receive baptism.

Might Peter, then or later, have remembered another Roman centurion—the man hailed by Jesus as showing more faith than any Israelite (Matthew 8:10)? The gospel of peace removes hostility and enables enemies to become friends.

6 Fight the good fight

Ephesians 6:10–18

The biblical passages we have explored this week indicate that peace is costly and far from passive. In a violent and divided world, only rugged and imaginative '*shalom* activism' offers a realistic alternative to the violent tactics touted as 'realistic' but discredited throughout history.

There is a war on! There are battles to be fought against oppression, injustice, greed and hatred. Those who refuse to accept the status quo, who long for a different reality, must fight for it. Those who refuse to defend an unjust global system, based on the threat of violence, that oppresses the poor so that a few can live in affluence, must challenge the powers that be. But we must take care that we are not co-opted by the powers we fight against.

We must identify the nature of the struggle, according to this dramatic passage from Ephesians. The enemy is not flesh and blood. If we fight against those who are made in God's image and for whom Christ died, we have misinterpreted the struggle and may find ourselves fighting on the wrong side. The real battle is against principalities and powers—spiritual forces that inhabit, distort and manipulate human structures, ideologies and institutions. Not the least of these is the nation-state, which demands unquestioning loyalty and repeated blood sacrifices.

If we would engage in what some have called 'the war of the Lamb' (see Revelation 17:14), we must put on the whole armour of God. If we would confront these malign powers, if we would persist until the system changes, and if we would not lose heart or become casualties of the struggle, we will need all the equipment listed here. One essential is 'the gospel of peace' (v. 15), the message that Peter brought to his enemy, Cornelius.

What is this message? God intends to reconcile the whole of creation so that *shalom* is universal. The prophets have given us tantalising glimpses of this vision. Jesus came to show us how to live towards it, to make peace between God and humanity and to break down the dividing walls between us (Ephesians 2:14). We are to pray for the coming of God's kingdom of justice and peace, embody its values as we love our enemies, and struggle peacefully against all that opposes God's purposes.

Guidelines

Christians disagree about issues of war and peace. Biblical texts are marshalled to justify different approaches and arguments. The passages we have explored this week are only a sample, selected to reflect the 'peace church' tradition. As the Christendom era gives way to post-Christendom and Christians find themselves rethinking ethical issues in a changing world, many conclude that the 'just war' approach is no longer credible. New ways of thinking are needed. The 'peace church' tradition suggests a starting point—a modest proposal for peace: 'Let the Christians of the world agree that they will not kill each other.' At the end of this week, you might reflect on the implications of this proposal.

As you pray:

- Rejoice in the reconciling love of God and the peace-making life, death and resurrection of Jesus.
- Ask for fresh insights into the biblical vision of *shalom* and how this might be realised in your community.
- Reflect on the 'modest proposal for peace' and pray for all who are caught up in situations where they might be asked to kill others.
- Pray for conflict zones, asking God to bring a just peace, and pray for those working for reconciliation.

FURTHER READING

Alan Kreider, Eleanor Kreider and Paulus Widjaja, *A Culture of Peace*, Good Books, 2005. Presents a biblical vision for churches that want to explore peace in many dimensions of life.

John Roth, *Choosing against War*, Good Books, 2002. An examination of biblical teaching on war and peace and advocacy of the 'peace church' tradition.

Willard Swartley, *Covenant of Peace*, Eerdmans, 2006. A discussion of almost all the references to peace in the New Testament.

Walter Wink, *Engaging the Powers*, Fortress, 1992. The third volume in a trilogy on 'the powers', exploring non-violent ways of engaging with injustice.

War and peace (II)

This year we commemorate the centenary of the start of the 'war to end war'. The last veterans have died and the village war memorials, with their tragic lists of the dead, are weathered with age, but war itself is not history and soldiers have not gone away. They don't normally wear uniform in church and the wars don't often reach the front pages of our newspapers, but there are military personnel in our families and in our churches, and there are more than 50 conflicts continuing in the world today. As Christians we must not simply ignore them or wish them away.

Maurice Wood DSO was Bishop of Norwich in the 1970s and 1980s, but on D Day, 1944, he was a 26-year-old commando-trained Naval Chaplain on the beaches of Normandy. Interviewed on the radio in 2004, he explained that the first wave of troops, who had arrived some 30 minutes earlier, were 'pinned down a bit, and there was a lot of firing going on'. Asked if the events of that day, caring for and praying with the many wounded men, had made him question his faith, he replied, 'Strangely enough, I must say quite simply, "No". I had a clear faith in Christ. I also read my Bible, and it was always full of wars and tumults and I was used to the fact that the Bible had a lot about war in it' (*Today*, Radio 4, 6 June 2004).

Over the next week we will look at some of the passages, and some of the men, he may have had in mind. From the Psalms we see God's concern to rescue and deliver the oppressed, and ask if we can ever say that God is on 'our side'. With Nehemiah we seek the practicalities of trusting God while under armed threat. In the Gospels we meet individual soldiers discovering what it means to act justly and to have faith in Christ. There and in the Acts of the Apostles we find the legions—the tough bodies of regular or auxiliary troops that formed a key part of the New Testament world. Together, these readings should help us to think through some of the realities of the use of armed force, and to pray for those in our armed services, in times of peace and of war.

Unless otherwise indicated, quotations are taken from the New International Version of the Bible.

1 Acting as God's agents

Psalm 82

Who are the 'gods' in verse 1 of this psalm? Some scholars identify them as spiritual beings—the heathen deities of Israel's neighbours or, more generally, the 'forces of evil' of Ephesians 6:12 (NRSV). Others say they are Israel's human judges, and cite Jesus' words in support: charged with blasphemy, 'because you, a mere man, claim to be God' (John 10:33), he quotes verse 6 of this psalm to defend himself, implying that the 'gods' here are also human. They are 'those to whom the word of God came' (John 10:35, NRSV)—Israel and, in particular, her judges, who should protect the weak and the oppressed (Psalm 82:3–4). This is God's own role (Exodus 22:22–24), so they act as his agents in defending the widow and the fatherless, a theme amplified by the prophets (for example, Isaiah 1:16–17).

Such work is both a privilege and an honour (in Psalm 82:6 these people are called 'sons of the Most High'), but here the judges are themselves judged. Their failure is not necessarily in bad actions, actively defending the unjust or showing partiality to the wicked. It is enough that they have done nothing for the vulnerable (v. 3) and have simply left the oppressed in the hands of wicked men. This is moral ignorance and blindness (v. 5), perfectly described in words attributed to Dietrich Bonhoeffer: 'Silence in the face of evil is itself evil: God will not hold us guiltless. Not to speak is to speak. Not to act is to act.'

According to the New Testament, the governing authorities have been appointed by God to maintain justice and peace in the world, and are to be prayed for and respected (Romans 13:1–7; 1 Timothy 2:2). In fighting justly, those wielding armed force today are standing in the line of the 'gods' of this psalm. Their mortality (v. 7) is a constant reminder that they may be 'gods' but they are not God. Humanly imposed justice will always be relative; injustice will not disappear until God himself finally judges the world (v. 8). In the meantime, however, doing nothing in the face of evil is not an option we should contemplate.

2 God on our side?

Psalm 18

Can soldiers ever claim that God is on their side? This psalm is found also in 2 Samuel 22, where it relates to the many conflicts within which David was entangled. The references to fighting on foot (vv. 29, 33) suggest that it is from David's time: later kings fought from chariots (1 Kings 22:34).

David's enemies in the psalm are not necessarily from another religion: he has faced rebellion from within his own kingdom as well as invasions by the pagan Philistines. Both he and his enemies have cried to the Lord for help (vv. 6, 41), so why has God answered only David's prayers? It is not simply that he is God's anointed king: he has been attacked by 'a violent man' (v. 48), perhaps his own son, Absalom, who rebelled against him (2 Samuel 15), and is acting with righteousness (v. 20). From the first words of the psalm, David has also humbled himself before God, recognising that God's power is greater than any military power (vv. 7–15) and that true strength is found as much in gentleness (the literal meaning of 'help' at the end of verse 35) as in brute force (v. 34).

David knows his dependence on God and his own fragility: in the rush of battle a twisted ankle (v. 36) or a failed attempt to jump a low wall (v. 29) can be as fatal as a wound from spear or arrow. This awareness, along with the immediacy of the danger (the Hebrew tense is of continuing action, which may even imply that the threat is not yet passed), leads to his exultation in victory (vv. 37–45). As Winston Churchill would express it, 'Nothing in life is so exhilarating as to be shot at without result' (Churchill, *The Story of the Malakand Field Force*, 1898, p. 107). David, however, adds a sense of deep gratitude to God who has given him his strength and preserved him, and this allows him to show mercy, sparing the jealous Saul (1 Samuel 24:4) and the stone-throwing Shimei (2 Samuel 16:5–13). When soldiers today share this attitude, they too can show mercy and exercise what another David (the US General David Petraeus) named 'courageous restraint'.

3 Keeping the peace

Nehemiah 2:1–16

The book of Nehemiah is recognised by even the most sceptical scholars as an authentic, if humanly self-serving, account of this Jewish soldier and leader. Given his role in the Persian court, he may have been a eunuch: if so, he would have been banned from the rebuilt Jewish temple (Deuteronomy 23:1), able to 'enter' it only through the medium of this book, deposited there as a formal record. But if his boastfulness (Nehemiah 5:19; 13:14) is unattractive, his dynamic leadership and practical faith lead to a major achievement. Jerusalem's rebuilt walls not only protected people and temple; they demonstrated imperial toleration for the worship of the Lord.

Nehemiah integrates faith in God and the use of military power: a heartfelt informal prayer (vv. 4–5) precedes his appeal to the emperor, and he happily takes supplies from the royal park (v. 8), as well as a Persian personal protection team to guard him during his journey and his night-time reconnaissance of Jerusalem's broken walls. The project provokes the threat of violent attack (4:8) or assassination (6:2), so he arms the people, not because he wants conflict but to prevent it. A military commander today, calling by radio for his Quick Reaction Force, would recognise Nehemiah's tactical wisdom in keeping fully half his force at immediate readiness to fight, and having his officers positioned strategically and his signaller constantly close by (4:13–20). He achieves his aim and there is no attack, but at the cost of grinding pressure: work continues from first to last light, and guards stand sentry even through the night.

There is a fascinating contrast between Nehemiah and his contemporary, Ezra the priest, whose own boast is of rejecting imperial security and relying only on God's direct protection (Ezra 8:22). Scripture does not allow us to decide arbitrarily that one is right and the other wrong: both are faithful; both rely on God. The challenge for us, and for our political leaders, is to know when to follow the one rather than the other.

4 'What should we soldiers do?'

Luke 3:1–14

Luke places John the Baptist's call within a layered and multinational framework of powers. Above the immediate context of first-century Judaism are the local client kings, ruling by force of arms. They in turn are backed by the overarching power of Tiberius Caesar and the legions—power embodied in Judea by the governor, Pontius Pilate. The mention of two high priests (v. 2) indicates the all-pervasive nature of Roman power: the high priesthood was supposed to be a lifetime appointment by the Sanhedrin but in AD15 Pilate's predecessor as governor had unilaterally removed Annas from the role. Annas retained influence but Caiaphas, his son-in-law, held the official title.

John's call is to all these groups, not just to Israel: 'all people will see God's salvation' (v. 6) through repentance and forgiveness (v. 3). His baptism signifies forgiveness and his teaching then offers practical ways in which a repentant attitude of mind will be shown.

Some find it astonishing that soldiers should have come to John (v. 14). Both Pharisees and early Christians generally regarded soldiering as, at best, a questionable profession and some theologians have argued against this passage's historicity because it allows the possibility of a military career. But it is hardly surprising that soldiers, both Jewish and Gentile, were among those who responded to John's message. Who would know better than they of the ethical challenges faced by those who bear and use arms? The thrust of their question is therefore 'What should we do when our duties seem to be at odds with Godly piety?' John does not tell them to abandon their profession but to avoid abusing force for personal gain. Just as in our own day, soldiers were not well paid, but they are to be content (the word means more than physical contentment) with their pay. They cannot collectively promote justice if, individually, they are acting unjustly. All who respond to John are called to a new generosity of heart (v. 11) but those who have more than usual power are called to more than usual repentance.

5 Learning faith and humility from a soldier

Luke 7:1–10

Some years ago, a theatre group produced a dramatised version of the parable of the good Samaritan (Luke 10:29–37) in which not only the standard social worker and vicar but also the predictable punk rocker passed by. It was the despised politician, returning from closing a local hospital, who stopped and helped the injured man. There is something of the same shock here, in the idea that the local synagogue leaders consider this centurion, probably a wealthy Gentile member of Herod Antipas' soldiery, worthy of Jesus' help. Despite our tendency to consider people as either complete saints or total sinners, the human reality is more nuanced. Luke leaves us unsure: this soldier may love, respect and honour his servant or he may simply value him for his financial worth. The word translated 'valued highly' (v. 2) has the same ambiguity in New Testament Greek as in English. But we can learn about humility from him, and about faith.

The centurion knows his unworthiness. Whether he himself meets Jesus (Matthew 8:5) or simply sends well-wishers on his behalf (Luke 7:3)—or indeed whether he first sent others before his concern overcame his reluctance and he went himself—his message is consistent: 'I am not worthy' (v. 7). Yet he asks Jesus for help because he understands authority (v. 8). In the military, even the most senior ranks can command only because they themselves are under higher command. This insight into the nature of faith is in the centurion's intuitive understanding that Jesus receives authority through his relationship to the Father, and therefore holds authority over the created world. Jesus' power over the servant's illness is delegated from the Father.

This is why 'mustard seed' faith (Luke 17:6) is enough, and Jesus does not need to be present physically. This unclean Gentile soldier's 'great faith' (7:9) is both a challenge and an encouragement to us to see our heavenly Father's glory in Jesus, and to let neither our unworthiness nor the depth of the issues we face prevent us from casting all our anxiety on God, because he cares for us (1 Peter 5:7).

6 Protecting life, preserving order

Acts 23:12–32

'Pray that I may be kept safe,' asks Paul in Romans 15:31. How does God answer such a prayer? The military garrison in Jerusalem has twice saved Paul's life already, rescuing him from a riotous mob outside the temple (Acts 21:32) and then pulling him from the midst of the Sanhedrin before he was torn asunder (23:10). Soldiers save his life a third time in today's reading, and will do so on at least two more occasions (25:3–5; 27:43) before Paul reaches Rome.

Faced with a conspiracy to assassinate Paul, the tribune acts decisively and bloodlessly to prevent it, sending infantry and heavy cavalry on a 35-mile forced march to the mainly Gentile area of Antipatris—a straightforward if tiring evolution for trained troops on roads and in the cool of the night. The overwhelming force of Paul's escort is, paradoxically, both proportionate force and minimum force, deterring violence by rendering any attempt at ambush futile.

These soldiers are not presented as paragons of virtue. Their concern is not especially for Paul (their commanding officer believes him to be an Egyptian terrorist, 21:38) but for good order: the ambush of a man in their custody is not to be permitted. Nor are the soldiers shown as models of gentleness. Only Paul's revelation of his protective Roman citizenship has prevented a violent interrogation (22:25): flogging frequently killed the victim.

The military profession, founded as it was on emperor worship, was immensely difficult for the first Christians. This makes the New Testament's sympathy to the military astonishing. But it was military power, threatened or used, that upheld the Pax Romana, which enabled the gospel to spread so quickly across the known world. Neither mobs nor plotters are susceptible to argument: Paul's life was saved by military 'strength and guile' (incidentally the motto of the Special Boat Service) and Paul saw God at work in such salvation: 'the Lord rescued me' (2 Timothy 3:11).

Guidelines

Even as we look back to the outbreak of World War I, armed conflicts continue across the world. The readings of the past week, and the many other military personnel, metaphors and events in the Bible's pages, can help us engage with the questions of justice and peace they raise. Christians in the military, as well as congregations in general, face difficult dilemmas in seeking to be faithful to the God of peace in a violent world. Perhaps this year is an especially appropriate time for churches to address these themes in sermons and study groups, recognising that we have sometimes treated them in simplistic or superficial ways. We may reap further benefits: if churches are increasingly feminised, then an understanding of the culture of the military world—masculine, and largely populated by men—can aid the task of becoming 'mission-shaped'.

Whatever our personal views on the morality of particular conflicts, we will surely wish to pray for those involved. This prayer, for all on operations, is adapted from a prayer for 40 Commando Royal Marines:

Lord Jesus Christ, who in the hour of your death were recognised as Saviour by a soldier standing nearby: be to all those on military operations a sign of saving hope during their deployment. Keep them steadfast and courageous in times of danger and ever-pressing fear; maintain their righteous and humane values, and uphold their good wills when tested; and keep them alert and skilled in their tasks, until they return to their families and loved ones. For your name's sake. Amen

Prayers in the Old Testament

The New Testament resounds with the prayers of people, influential and ordinary, pious and of dubious morality. They occur frequently and are certainly a vital source for nourishing our Christian formation. But there are many significant and developmental prayers also in the Old Testament. The natural place to look for them would be the Psalms, but the selection over the next fortnight intentionally leaves them aside. Instead, we shall be reflecting on prayers associated with important characters in the developing story of the Old Testament and/or occurring at important moments in that story. They provide us with many fascinating examples and stimulation to pray.

Although we shall consider these prayers in the chronological order in which they are presented within the Bible, we can also recognise that they would have resonated with God's people at many times in their unfolding history. Do be alert to these 'secondary' functions, even though we do not have the space to focus heavily upon them. The recognition that these prayers would have spoken to people throughout Israel's journey affirms us in seeking to use them to shape and sharpen our own praying.

It is noteworthy that Chris Wright, in his highly significant book *The Mission of God: Unlocking the Bible's grand narrative* (IVP, 2006), pays little attention to the role of prayers such as these in the unfolding of that narrative. This is not to criticise the book, but simply to suggest that paying attention to the way that prayer is threaded through the 'grand narrative' is a worthwhile task. That is true, I believe, not only from an informative perspective but also for our own spiritual transformation. If we are to play our part in God's mission today, we need to grasp the privilege and importance of prayer as one medium through which God carries out his mission.

Quotations are taken from the New Revised Standard Version of the Bible.

1 Abraham: lingering before God

Genesis 18:16–33

Prayer takes many forms but at the heart of it is a conversation with God. On this understanding, Abraham's controversy with God over the fate of Sodom and its people is prayer, even though it is not so described.

Embedded within this prayer narrative is a critical issue, namely the balance between the ungodliness that brings God's destructive judgment and the righteousness that might avert it. Which is the stronger force or carries the greater weight within God's scheme? This question was a vital concern for God's people as they reflected on the fall of Jerusalem and the exile into Babylon. Clearly there were righteous people in the land at the time, including Ezekiel, Jeremiah and, presumably, Baruch, Jeremiah's scribe—but God's judgment still fell on the nation. It had relevance, a few years earlier, to the good King Josiah, who instigated many righteous reforms but still died in battle, and it is a difficult issue for many today. The Christian understanding of Jesus indicates that one perfect person may atone for untold multitudes of sinful ones.

Also embedded within this narrative is another fundamental question asked by most people who pray: what difference does prayer make? At one level, the answer given here could be 'Not a lot!' God discerns that Sodom should be destroyed because of its wickedness, and destroyed it is (Genesis 19:24–25), despite Abraham's pleas. Mixed with the judgment is God's mercy: Lot, his wife, his daughters and their husbands-to-be are given the opportunity to escape the destruction. Yet his wife and sons-in-law, through their own choices, perish. Soon afterwards, Lot's daughters involve him in a devastating scandal (19:36) and Lot himself fades from the narrative of redemption.

Nevertheless, Abraham provides a model for prophetic intercession. God chooses to inform him, to take him into his confidence about his plans for the future, because Abraham is involved with God in his redemptive purposes (vv. 18–19). With the angels (God's alter ego) gone to search Sodom, 'Abraham remained standing before the Lord' (v. 22).

This is the privileged position of those who will pray—a very risky position and role to have, but also, as the narrative indicates, a fruitful one. Although God could not save the city, he did answer Abraham's prayer (v. 25).

2 A servant's prayers

Genesis 24:1–14

Often in the Old Testament the prayers we are privileged to encounter are those made by the great names—the A list, so to speak, such as Abraham and Moses. There are, however, some less noticeable people who provide valuable insights about prayer and can encourage us all to explore and develop our prayer life further.

The person in today's story remains anonymous. He is only Abraham's servant—the senior servant ('the oldest of his house', v. 2), but still nameless. Yet this servant has a pivotal role in enabling the mission of God through Abraham to be carried out. He is the one appointed to find a wife for Isaac from Abraham's own kindred. This is a critical moment in the unfolding story of Abraham. The servant feels the burden of responsibility, so he will not swear the oath lightly but engages in debate with Abraham about the conditions for its fulfilment and his release from it (vv. 5–8).

The prayer story here is in three significant parts. We shall consider the first now and the other two in tomorrow's reading.

Part one is a prayer made at a critical moment in the unfolding drama (vv. 12–14). Its position here indicates the attitude of Abraham's servant: all that he does, he does in dependence on God. Yes, he has used his own initiative, he has prepared for the task entrusted to him and he recognises the opportunity presented by the evening camel-watering. He has invested himself in the risky and arduous journey to Nahor. There is no suggestion that this man regards prayer as an alternative to committed service, but he knows that real 'success' is totally dependent on God (v. 12) and so he asks for it.

It is also clear that he does not seek success for his own satisfaction. At the centre of his prayer request is God's mission through Abraham. The reference to 'steadfast love' in verses 12 and 14 is shorthand for the covenant promises given to Abraham in Genesis 12:1–3; 15:4–5 and 17:3–8, namely the promises of offspring, the land of Canaan and blessing for the whole world. The positioning of the words 'show steadfast love' at the beginning and end of the prayer underlines that this is the core issue.

3 Waiting in prayer

Genesis 24:15–52

Verses 26–27 present us with the second great prayer of this anonymous servant. This too is remarkable for several reasons.

The prayer is a blessing. It is quite understandable that the servant should wish to bless the Lord, because God has answered his prayer to direct him to the right woman. By her hospitable response she has met his conditions as to how God would indicate the right girl to become Isaac's wife, and her family history has confirmed that she is of Abraham's kindred. But what is so amazing about it?

To pray this blessing at this point in the drama requires considerable faith. As the narrative continues, we learn that there are many other steps to be completed before the 'wife for Isaac' is secured. Yet, by blessing God, the servant is assuming, in faith, that the details will work out. Secondly, we notice again the phrase 'steadfast love'. This is the focus of the man's actions and prayers. Again, his concern is primarily for the fulfilment of God's mission. Next comes his concern for Abraham ('my master' is mentioned three times in the prayer) and finally his own 'satisfaction': 'The Lord has led me…'.

There is much here to serve as a model for prayer, but even more to offer an example of the ideal disposition of those who pray. Here is someone who, in the words of Jesus, 'seeks first God's kingdom'. This committed attitude is indicated even before his extended conversation with the girl. Having spent weeks travelling to get to this critical encounter and making his initial approach, 'The man gazed at her in silence to learn whether or not the Lord had made his journey successful' (v. 21).

The servant clearly has many resources at his disposal to persuade the girl (and her father) to agree to the marriage, but neither his resources nor his resourcefulness is the critical factor. It is his life of prayer.

The servant's prayerful disposition is reinforced by the centrality of prayer throughout the story. As the servant encounters Rebekah's's father and explains his mission to him (making this a priority before his own needs and comforts, v. 33), his prayerful approach is reiterated (vv. 42–44, 48; see also v. 52), and it is this testimony to prayer that convinces Laban (v. 51). Clearly prayer contributes vitally to this part of God's unfolding mission.

4 Moses: prayer as mission

Exodus 33:12—34:12

The people of God are on a journey from Egypt to the promised land. Having experienced God's deliverance, they are involved by God in fulfilling the promises given to the patriarchs. They are a people on a mission, but they are also a flawed people, having entered into idolatry and deception (31:18—32:35). In today's verses we see Moses engaged in prayer in the context of restoring the Israelites to the mission of God for them.

Firstly, in 33:12–16, Moses engages with God to ensure that God remains at the heart of all that he and his people do and are. Robert Warren, in his book *Being Human, Being Church* (HarperCollins, 1995), has pointed out that one of the dangers for churches as they move into mission mode is that they can become like ring doughnuts—with a hollow core (pp. 63–65). This prayer illustrates Moses' passion for God to remain at the core of his leadership and the people's mission. He 'cashes in' the commitment of God to him that he has 'found favour in [your] sight', and he asks that God would 'show me your ways' (v. 13). This means far more than just 'Please reveal your plans to me.' As God's response in verses 17–23 makes clear, it is about God showing Moses who God is. If the church is going to keep its centre from becoming hollow, it needs leaders who recognise that they need to keep intimate time with God and to discover all of God that they can. This may involve study, but it also requires revelation from God that comes through prayerfully seeking him above all things.

Secondly, Moses seeks forgiveness and renewal for himself and his people, so that they can continue to fulfil God's mission. Again, he prays out of his relationship with God: 'If [or 'since'] I have found favour in your sight…' (34:9). He acknowledges the reality of his people's attitude (and perhaps his own feelings towards them): they are 'a stiff-necked people'. Then he seeks forgiveness on their behalf—but also identifies himself with them ('pardon *our* iniquity'). Finally he asks God to claim them and give them a future: 'take us for your inheritance'. Here are some key principles for prayer in a missional context, and all of this flows out of the leader's worship experience (34:8).

5 Naomi: blessing and history-shaping

Ruth 1:1–20

Naomi is unlikely to spring to mind as one of the great 'prayer makers' of the Old Testament—indeed, she does not seem to exemplify many great attributes at all—but here in verses 8–9 there are two blessings. Blessings are of two main kinds: there are those in which people bless God and those in which they ask God to bless others. It is the latter kind that we have here. As Naomi, full of grief and bitterness, prepares to return to Bethlehem, she gives fairly standard blessings to the daughters-in-law who are being left behind in Moab.

We might dismiss these 'prayers' on three counts. First, they are not prayers in structure: they don't address God directly; second, they are routine rather than profound; and third, Naomi gives no indication that she really expects God to fulfil them. They are hardly full of dynamic faith—and yet we should look closer.

It is understandable that Naomi's faith in God was not cutting-edge. The land that God had promised would flow with milk and honey had turned into a place of famine, so her family had migrated to Moab to find food. There her husband and two sons had died, leaving her bereft and vulnerable. Her planned return to Bethlehem to find sustenance with her kin meant that she would lose her companions in life and sorrow, her daughters-in-law. God had not been good to her. So, rather than dismissing these blessings as superficial or ritualistic, we can see that, for Naomi, uttering them cost her a lot.

Once spoken, the blessings shape the rest of the narrative. While it is impossible for Naomi to supply her daughters-in law with replacement husbands (vv. 11–13), it is not impossible for God to respond to Naomi's prayer by finding a truly caring husband for the loyal Ruth (see 4:13) and, in the process, ensuring Naomi's well-being (4:15–16).

More significantly for us, as we keep our eye on the missional impact of prayer, is the ultimate consequence of the blessings. Ruth and Boaz are gifted with a son, Obed, who will be 'the father of Jesse, the father of David' (4:17). The rest is, as we might say, 'history'. More than that, it is the unfolding purpose of God in history, the pathway to the world's redemption—and all because an old, broken woman dared to utter a plea to God to bless others, in these two 'prayers'.

6 Hannah: divine partnership

1 Samuel 1:9–20; 2:1–10

Hannah's prayers, like Naomi's, are concerned with her own immediate family relationships (especially her childlessness and the pressure it puts on her relationship with her husband) but they are integral to the mission of God's people.

Because of her childlessness and the taunts of her husband's other wife, Hannah 'was deeply distressed and prayed to the Lord, and wept bitterly' (1:10). Her prayer took the form of a vow—a plea to God, accompanied by a promise. Before we are tempted to condemn this kind of praying as sub-Christian (perhaps we might see it as an attempt to twist God's arm), we should recall that sometimes God puts his prayers into us for us to pray out.

This prayer is prayed to the God Hannah knows: 'O Lord of Hosts' (v. 11); and it springs out of her committed relationship to God, for it is made in the temple at Shiloh, where Hannah was a regular worshipper. Furthermore, she trusts God enough to share her deep distress with him. This was no easy prayer: it was spoken with desperate tears, and the consequences for Hannah—the surrender of a firstborn son back to God—were clearly not a light commitment. In the depth of her distress, it resembles the prayer of Jesus in Gethsemane.

Eli's response can act as a reminder to those of us who lead, of how easily we can misjudge people. Praying without speaking the words aloud was strange, as, until relatively recently, was reading silently. Hannah was moving her lips 'but her voice was not heard' (1:13), so Eli misreads Hannah's activity as a sign of drunkenness. This is particularly ironic when we remember that Hannah was dedicating any son that God might grant her to total abstinence. To his credit, however, Eli listens to her carefully and accepts her explanation.

Hannah's second prayer (2:1–10) contrasts markedly with her first. It is a song of exaltation, full of rich liturgical phraseology. This reminds us of the value of using the resources of the faith community to express our relationship to God. Many see echoes of this prayer in Mary's song of praise to God, in Luke 1:47–55.

Although Hannah's prayers came out of an intensely personal situation, they were used by God to provide the nation with the great prophet Samuel, furthering his mission with and through his people.

Guidelines

Which of these prayers (or praying people) offer you the greatest help? Perhaps you can see some parallel between their situation and yours; they might offer you insights into the deep reality of prayer, or maybe you even find their prayers problematic.

There are special places for prayer mentioned in these passages—for example, the temple at Shiloh, or the holy mountain at Sinai. For Christians, there may also be special places that help to stabilise us in a crisis and facilitate our prayers. In the light of John 4:22–24, however, where Jesus indicates that special places will be replaced by our relationship with God in the Spirit, and of Jeremiah's strictures about wrongly depending on special 'holy' places (7:1–12), what are the potential dangers in them?

How might we use the insights about the place of prayer in leadership and mission from the Old Testament within our own context and for the benefit of our own churches? What adaptations and adjustments do we need to make, bearing in mind that these are 'old covenant' prayers?

1 Elijah: spiritual warfare and vulnerability

1 Kings 18:36–40; 19:1–10

These two passages reflect very different aspects of Elijah's relationship with God in prayer. The first is very public as he stands exposed in conflict with Ahab, Jezebel and the 400 prophets of Baal; in the second he is alone before God. The first concerns a far-reaching conflict about the power of the gods and the control of fertility, behind which lurk profound issues relating to consumerism, creation and the nature of religion itself, while the second seems deeply personal and almost pathetic. In the first, Elijah struts the stage as a Titan; in the second, he is dwarfed and feeble. The prayers are linked, however, not only by the mountains on which they take place and the mission that generates both, but also as illustrations of the vulnerability of leaders.

In 1 Kings 18, Elijah's own future was at stake: if the challenge had gone in favour of the Baal prophets, he would have been slaughtered. The destiny of Israel was also endangered: if Baalism had been victorious, it may well have overwhelmed Yahwism and, with it, the identity of God's people. It was, physically and spiritually, a life-or-death moment. 1 Kings 19 reveals Elijah's own vulnerabilities and self-doubts. (Some would see in it his proneness to depression, but this is not the kind of vulnerability I have in mind.)

Both prayers show us clearly that, as Christian leaders, involved with God's people in furthering God's mission, we are totally dependent on God. Elijah did a lot of negotiation and organisation to bring the trial by sacrifice to a head (see 18:17–19, 30–35), from engaging Ahab, setting up the trial and gathering his people to rebuilding the altar and preparing the materials for the sacrifice—but then he was totally dependent on God. What if God did not answer by fire? Therefore, prayer was primary in his missional leadership.

Afterwards, Elijah's own sanity was equally dependent upon God: he was personally and spiritually extremely vulnerable. If God had not provided, he would never have made it to his next divine appointment. If

God had not initiated the healing with the question 'What are you doing here, Elijah?' or met him in and after the 'sound of sheer silence' (19:12), Elijah would have been lost. But Elijah's God, and ours, is a God who answers both by public fire and personal embrace.

2 Hezekiah: surrender to God

2 Kings 19:8–20, 32–37

Jerusalem was in the utmost jeopardy. The Assyrian army, having devastated much of Judah and drained the country of resources, was now besieging Jerusalem. Having taunted Hezekiah (18:19–25), even claiming that he was doing so with Hezekiah's God's approval, the Rabshakeh (an army commander) delivered his ultimatum not to the king but directly to the people, appealing to them to surrender (18:29–35). This made Hezekiah extremely vulnerable. Not only was there an all-conquering and vicious army outside, but insurrection within his city was now probable. It doesn't get much tougher for any leader.

The natural response to such an attack is either to strike out at the people around or to panic, crumble and try to run away or hide from reality. Hezekiah's strategy, however, was to pray.

In 2 Kings 19, having read a further threatening letter from the king of Assyria, he first 'went up to the house of the Lord and spread it before the Lord' (v. 14). Both steps are significant. He goes to the place where he is closest to God, where, historically, God has been worshipped and has made himself known to people like the great King Solomon. Here God's promises have been received and celebrated. Then he spreads the letter before the Lord. In other words, he intentionally brings the hard world of militarism, devious politics and statecraft into the searchlight of God's presence. There is no aspect of human life that cannot be brought to God. In opening the letter before God, he is inviting God into the total situation. There is no attempt to cover up or pretend, either to himself or to God.

Finally, he prays—and what an amazing prayer it is. He affirms God's special relationship with Israel, he grasps the overarching power of God as Creator, he shows his concern for God's honour as well as his clear awareness of Sennacherib's military might, and he appeals to God to rescue them all. Here there is much to commend to us as a pattern for our petitions and intercessions.

God's response is to assure him through the prophet's words and then to act to fulfil them.

3 Jeremiah: missional exhaustion

Jeremiah 15:10–21

One of the roles of a prophet was to intercede, yet Jeremiah has been commanded by God to stop praying for the welfare of his people (see 11:14; 14:11). In the end, Jeremiah would suffer the same fate as them, seeing Jerusalem sacked and the temple desecrated, then being taken captive and probably executed. In many ways, Jeremiah's call from God caused him intense isolation (15:15, 17), and he also shared the nation's rejection by God. No wonder Jeremiah has been seen as an Old Testament exemplar of the suffering Christ (Robinson, *The Cross in the Old Testament*, pp. 119–173). He feels as if God has failed him, like a river that dries up when it is most needed.

Against this background, we can understand his cry in 15:10, 'Woe is me…'. This is no superficial complaint. It expresses a perception that he has been cursed. Just as the land and people are cursed by God because they have broken God's covenant, so Jeremiah shares their doom. Perhaps this explains the strange passage in verses 13–14 (see also 17:1–4, especially v. 3), where God seems to address Jeremiah as though he were condemned Israel.

God's response to Jeremiah's cries is not a soft one. Yes, he is with Jeremiah 'to save you and deliver you' (v. 21), but this is a conditional promise ('if you turn back…', v. 19) and it will require God to make Jeremiah like a 'fortified wall of bronze' (v. 20). The struggle is going to be long, intense and very hard.

Jeremiah would later be delivered from the prison pit (38:7–13); in the end, God's people would be saved through the fire of exile (ch. 29) and there would be a new covenant (31:31–37), but the prophet pays a high price. His prayer models honest encounter with God but offers us no easy solutions (consider also Mark 14:32–42). Sometimes—perhaps most times, to one degree or another—living for the mission of God will involve us in suffering. Jeremiah helps us prepare for that and live through it. He even helps when we feel we can't cope any longer.

4 Nehemiah: resource for mission

Nehemiah 1:1—2:4

Nehemiah may stick in our minds as the man who got the job done— rebuilding the walls of Jerusalem and, through that activity, re-establishing God's people as a religious force with their own identity. He has often served as an instructive model for leadership, but beyond and within all this is the story of his prayers and, hence, his relationship with God. He is remembered for his short 'arrow' prayers in critical moments, but these prayers reveal his grounding in a fertile, complex and costly spirituality.

The main prayer in today's passage is one of confession, as verse 6 notes. There are two main observations to make. First, the prayer appears formal and formulaic. It is well structured, with an address to God, an appeal to God, confession of sin and the recall of God's historic promise (here relating to Moses), followed by an appeal for restoration. It uses well-known words and phrases that have a Deuteronomic ring to them, from the 'God who keeps covenant' (v. 5) and his 'commandments, statutes and ordinances' (v. 7) through to 'if you return to me' (v. 9) and many other examples. It would be easy, therefore, to dismiss this as a ritualistic prayer—but there is another side.

The prayer comes from a person who has been deeply moved, involved in days of weeping, mourning and fasting. In doing this, he could well have been risking his own life: if the Babylonian king had caught wind of it, he could have had Nehemiah executed (see 2:2). Further, within the prayer is a personal dimension: Nehemiah confesses Israel's sin but also his family's and his own (v. 6). The conclusion of the prayer is not an expression of some general aspiration but a very particular request, seeking to gain the favour of a foreign king to benefit God's people (v. 11). There is a clear sense that Nehemiah is throwing himself into God's hands, exemplifying Proverbs 3:5–6. In this prayer we can see, at a deep level, a fusion of the riches of liturgical prayer with costly, personal commitment.

Nehemiah was an effective leader who accomplished a near-impossible task. He was pragmatic but he was equally prayerful. One of his challenges to us is to live a life in which prayer is just as thoroughly integrated into our personal and public life, so that we can be as effective as he was.

5 Jonah: struggling with God's mission

Jonah 4

When you get to heaven, how would you feel if you found that Hitler and Saddam Hussein were also there? Would you be perplexed that such notoriously evil human beings could be allowed to enjoy everlasting bliss, or would you be overwhelmed by the all-sufficiency of God's redeeming love in Christ? Perhaps you would be so shocked that you wouldn't know what to think.

This is the kind of struggle at the heart of the book of Jonah, and it comes to a head in this prayer. The original readers of the book knew that Nineveh was a cruel nation—not only in general but also against God's people in particular. We can experience the feeling of horror that Nineveh generated by reading the book of Nahum. Nineveh should surely have received the harshest of punishments from God.

As the first verses of Jonah's prayer remind us, he had tried to avoid the commission to go to the Ninevites and call them to repentance, in case they actually received forgiveness. Now his worst fears have come true: God's abounding love has won them over, so they have escaped scot free, and Jonah's prayer is 'O Lord, please take my life from me' (v. 3).

Sometimes God's call to us can cut right across our human instincts. We are commanded to love our enemies, to forgive those who persecute us (Matthew 5:44). We might be asked to do something similar to what Peter feared—eating with unclean Gentiles (Acts 10). God's call might also mean changing career or moving home when we would prefer to stay put. How can we pray when we are in such struggles, and maybe feeling ashamed?

Jonah's prayer shows us that we can be completely honest. Even if, from our perspective, his complaint about God's generosity seems absurd, he was close enough to God to be straightforward in sharing his theological perplexities and his personal angst.

The God who loves the whole world also loves us when we struggle with his call, and he answers us. This prayer conversation exemplifies the ways in which God may respond. He throws back a verbal challenge—'Is it right for you to be angry? (v. 4)—but he also enables Jonah to explore the issues through his own experience, which acts to him as a parable. Through this, God shows Jonah that he does share the divine compassion: he can feel compassion even for a plant.

6 Habakkuk: sustaining faith

Habakkuk 3

If Jonah's view was that God had acted too vigorously and compassionately to save a totally evil nation, Habakkuk's was that God was not acting decisively or quickly enough to rescue his people from a violent and evil oppressor (see ch. 1). Many of us may feel closer to Habakkuk!

The prayer in chapter 3 is helpful for us as we seek to invest ourselves in God's mission. The more we allow ourselves to become identified with God's mission, the more difficult it may be for us to tolerate everything around us that is alien to God and defies his purposes. This difficulty can take the form of theological questions about theodicy (the problem of evil), or existential dilemmas caused by witnessing diseases such as cancer or motor neuron disease destroying our loved ones. It can manifest itself as frustration that our churches are so inward-looking and out of tune with the heart of God, or as a creeping paralysis when we see injustice and violence destroying peoples and nations.

One way to handle these situations is to withdraw ourselves from the heart of God's mission, to settle for less pain, to invest less effort in partnering with God in his mission and to distract ourselves with other passions, but Habakkuk's prayer suggests an alternative therapy.

First, he relives and rekindles his awareness of God's great redemptive acts. He does this liturgically as he recites or sings the triumphant psalm in verses 1–15. The words 'I have heard of your renown…' (v. 2) may be seen as an expression of creedal faith, but they are far more than that, because they are a prayer, directed not to himself or his community but to God. Habakkuk expresses his reverence for God and his deep longing for the things of God—but the liturgical experience is also important as it nourishes him deep in his spirit.

Having been nourished by his prayer, he makes a great leap of faith into the arms of God: 'Though the fig tree does not blossom... I will exult in the God of my salvation' (vv. 17–18). Sometimes, being faithful to God's mission requires us to bear faithfully the pain of apparent failure and to continue hoping in God.

Guidelines

Several of these prayers reflect the struggles that we experience as people who are commissioned for or committed to the service of God in his mission. For most of us, there are times when the enormous privilege that we know this to be can weigh us down.

Reflect on the various responses to these struggles that the prayers offer. Do you find yourself identifying with one particular situation or response? Can you clarify for yourself why this might be?

Exhaustion in mission is not only an Old Testament phenomenon. If you recognise that this is part of your own condition, it may be helpful to reflect on the honesty of some of these prayers. Do they also indicate some of the ways that God can sustain us in our weakness?

If this is not a problem to you at the moment, perhaps it would be appropriate to spend time praying for those who are weary, confused or depressed.

FURTHER READING

H. Wheeler Robinson, *The Cross in the Old Testament*, SCM, 1955.
Christopher J.H. Wright, *The Mission of God*, IVP, 2006.

Supporting Messy Church
with a gift in your will

For many charities, income from legacies is crucial in enabling them to plan ahead, and often provides the funding to develop new projects. Legacies make a significant difference to the ability of charities to achieve their purpose. In just this way, a legacy to support BRF's ministry would make a huge difference.

One of the fastest growing areas of BRF is its Messy Church ministry (www.messychurch.org.uk). Messy Church is a form of church focused on building relationships, engaging with people outside the usual church context and building a Christ-centred community. Messy Church gives families and all age groups an opportunity to be together and is a congregation in its own right. In addition, it is being delivered in a variety of different contexts in local communities, including care homes, prisons, inner cities, schools and rural areas. Week by week we are seeing new Messy Churches starting up across the UK and around the globe, across all major Christian denominations. A conservative estimate is that over 250,000 people are attending Messy Church each month.

Throughout its history, BRF's ministry has been enabled thanks to the generosity of those who have shared its vision and supported its work, both by giving during their lifetime and also through legacy gifts.

A legacy gift would help fund the development and sustainability of BRF's Messy Church ministry into the future. We hope you may consider a legacy gift to help us continue to take this work forward in the decades to come.

For further information about making a gift to BRF in your will or to discuss how a specific bequest could be used to develop our ministry, please contact Sophie Aldred (Head of Fundraising) or Richard Fisher (Chief Executive) by email at fundraising@brf.org.uk or by phone on 01865 319700.

The BRF

Magazine

h+ for *Guidelines*

David Spriggs

Christians deserve better: better insights, better resources, better equipping and empowering so they can discover again the potency of the Bible.

'Guidelines readers are among the most committed and intelligent readers of the Bible, with a significant passion to engage with it, understand it more deeply and apply it to their lives, both personal and public.' This is an assumption, I know, but it is one to which I hold until proved wrong. I wonder if you agree with me.

If so, then I am sure you will want to know more about a substantial course, which Bible Society has been developing for five years or more.

h+ is the name of the course! The '*h*' stands first for 'how', for the course is about helping us understand how we read the Bible and how we can read it better. This is not just for our own sake but so that we can share the Bible's insights with others in everyday conversations as well as home groups and teaching. More formally, that process of understanding how we read written texts is called 'hermeneutics'—so the '*h*' also stands for this!

In fact, every time any of us reads the Bible, we are involved in the process of hermeneutics, whether we know it or not. Hermeneutics at its simplest means 'interpretations'. The Greek word is used in the story of Jesus interpreting the scriptures to the two disciples on the Emmaus road (Luke 24:27). Each time we read the Bible, a process goes on in our minds to seek to make sense of the 'signs' (which we normally think of as words but which also include the layout, capitalisation, paragraphs and punctuation) on the page in such a way as to make meaning out of the signs. Most of the time we do this quite unconsciously, but becoming more aware of the processes and resources involved in doing it well can be helpful to us and others. When we read the *Guidelines* notes provided by our writers, we do the same with what they have written, but, equally, they will have been involved in a conscious process of hermeneutics as they have read and interpreted the Bible to help us.

During recent decades, biblical scholars have invested much energy in 'biblical hermeneutics' and we at Bible Society felt it was high time that some of this expertise was made available to everyone who reads the Bible.

So what does *h+* offer, how does it work and who needs it?

What does *h+* offer?

Firstly, *h+* offers a first-class experience. *h+* gives everyone the opportunity to read the Bible better and to help others do the same. It is aimed at 'ordinary readers'—non-specialist, non-theologically trained Christians. It is based on extensive research about Bible needs and has been piloted and revised several times. So although it is a new product it has been thoroughly tested. It has been developed by Dr Andrew Rogers, an academic who has specialised in understanding the Bible needs of ordinary Christians, alongside a specialist trainer and a team of Bible Society people who understand the situation in our churches.

h+ offers three kinds of quality resources.

- a guide for the facilitator and a handbook for each participant. These materials are well laid out and engaging.
- a DVD for use in a computer (and, with larger groups, a data projector); PowerPoint presentations (one for each session); video clips of scholars explaining some of the trickier points (Tom Wright, Paula Gooder and Chris Wright), and humorous sketches, one for each session.
- a website providing extra support, which will continue to be developed.

How does *h+* work?

h+ runs as a ten-session course (about 1.5 hours per session), although the sessions can be combined to make, say, two full-day courses. Bible Society trains a facilitator (usually on a full-day course) who leads the ten sessions. The facilitator's training fee of £50 includes a full set of the resources, and the cost is subsidised by Bible Society. Lists of dates and venues are on the website.

The ten sessions cover topics such as understanding how we read the Bible, developing awareness of our personal and denominational perspectives, controversial issues like the creation account in Genesis chapter 1 and 'non-violence in Jesus' teaching, the conquest of Canaan and feminism, then insights into how the Bible is constructed as well as literary techniques in the ancient world and the reasons why translations may differ.

Underlying all the sessions are four key elements. Firstly, helping people understand the three worlds of the text: the historical context, the reader's context and how these viewpoints interact. Secondly (and this is the 'plus' in *h+*), following Richard Briggs, a focus on the 'virtuous reader', with one virtue each for most sessions (making it also a discipleship course). Thirdly, tackling biblical issues that are particularly troublesome for many today. Finally, increasing the participants' confidence in their ability to make good sense of the Bible, even the challenging parts.

h+ uses an apprenticeship model. The facilitator helps participants grow in understanding and confidence in engaging with the Bible; h+ is structured intentionally to involve participants at every step, and two sessions are run by the participants themselves, so that, by the end, they can pass on their learning and enjoyment to others: *h+* is also about the mission of the church.

Who needs *h+*?

Most preachers and Bible teachers need *h+*. It helps them to share their learning in a positive and beneficial way with their congregations.

Those with a responsibility to guide others as they engage with the Bible need it. It is ideal for Anglican Readers, as well as those who lead small groups, have pastoral responsibilities, teach RE in schools or take part in assemblies, or are involved in the children's and young people's work in a church.

Everyone needs it! Not all may need to go on the course, but all in a church, over time, will benefit as they hear the Bible read better, hear sermons that are more richly grounded in the scriptures, are helped with their problems and so on. We know that h+ leads to better Bible engagement and greater confidence in using the Bible—the churches' key text—everywhere.

Some quotes from users

- 'I want to use *h+* in our church to give people tools to understand and apply scripture for themselves.' (Cliff)
- 'I'll use it to help Christians I coach to use the Bible intelligently in their lives at work.' (Jill)
- 'I was impressed by its ability to treat the "ordinary reader" as a thinking being—it stretches the participants and asks them to think for themselves—and its clear stress on the process of biblical engagement.' (Stephen Lyon, coordinator of the Anglican Communion's *Bible in the Life of the Church* project)

For more information, including how to access one of the training events, see www.hplus.org.uk.

David Spriggs is Commissioning Editor of Guidelines *and Dean of Studies at Bible Society.*

Celebrating 25 years of ministry

Richard Fisher

In October 1988, Richard Fisher, BRF's Chief Executive, joined BRF. We asked him to reflect on the past 25 years.

What led you to work for BRF?

I was looking for something to do for a year between completing my university degree and going off to theological college. A friend mentioned that BRF was considering appointing a Field Officer for a one-year project; it sounded interesting so I applied and got the job. It was a great privilege to travel the length and breadth of the UK, introducing the work of BRF to some and reintroducing it to others—and that 'year off' has turned into 25 so far…

When BRF moved from London to Oxford in 1991, you became Chief Executive. What vision did you have for the organisation then?

I felt strongly, as others before me had done, that BRF was much more than just another Christian publisher. I wanted people to think of BRF more as a 'movement' seeking to resource the spiritual life and growth of individuals and congregations. I was asked in 1993 to set out a strategy for taking BRF forward and, while preparing this, I read all the minute books of BRF Trustee meetings dating back to 1922, when BRF started in St Matthew's Church, Brixton. I came to realise that what I thought was my fresh vision for BRF was, in fact, a rediscovery of the original vision of its founder, Canon Leslie Mannering.

What have been the highlights for you in the past 25 years?

There have been many! The establishment and growth of Barnabas Children's Ministry; the launch of Foundations21 as the first online discipleship resource of its kind, and, more recently, being the first in the UK to make our Bible reading notes available as apps for iPhones and iPads; Messy Church and Who Let The Dads Out? becoming part of BRF and growing from local church initiatives to national (and, for Messy Church, international) movements. Then there's been the thrill of seeing individual books occasionally published in unexpected languages—Arabic, Romanian, Ukrainian, Chinese, Afrikaans—and the interest that was generated in the secular media by our publication of *The Bible in Cockney*.

There have also been many memorable events—BRF's service of thanksgiving in Westminster Abbey in 1997, taking part in the pageants to mark The Queen Mother's 90th and 100th birthdays, and a BRF reception at Lambeth Palace in 2007 stand out as particular highlights.

BRF has expanded significantly in the past years. What factors do you believe have contributed to this growth?

Without doubt, BRF's greatest asset is its staff team, and I never cease to marvel at the way in which, so often, God has brought the right person to us at the right time. BRF has evolved organically over the years, often in ways that have taken us by surprise. I have no doubt that God has a plan for BRF and it's up to us to respond to the opportunities he has given to us. Looking back, one thing has often seemed to lead to another in the way BRF's ministries have developed.

In 2002, the BRF Council of Trustees approved a statement of purpose—'resourcing your spiritual journey'—which sums up what BRF is about. Everything we do relates to this purpose. Although our core ministries may, at first sight, seem to be quite different from one another, they complement and add value to one another in many ways. It really does all fit together and therein lies one of our main strengths.

There are two other very significant factors I must mention. One is the fantastic group of Trustees that we have at BRF, whose support, wisdom and encouragement have been key to our ability to take up the opportunities we have been given. The other is the trusts, churches and individuals whose financial support has made all the development possible. I am constantly amazed and humbled by their generosity to BRF.

Looking ahead, what is your vision for BRF in the next few years and your ministry within the organisation?

My vision is for BRF to continue enabling, equipping and resourcing others, both in their ministries/roles and in their own personal journeys of faith and discipleship. I don't want to make them dependent on BRF, but rather to help them to discover and exercise their own gifts. I hope we'll continue to be flexible and responsive to whatever new opportunities God gives us. I believe he still has work for me to do at BRF and I rather suspect that what started as a 'year off' could possibly turn out to be a life's work. But only God knows the answer to that!

Recommended reading

Kevin Ball

One of the joys of writing this section of the BRF Magazine is to know that, for many of you, these reviews are valued as a source for discovering good books. This time we have two new authors for BRF who have already thrilled readers with their earlier books published elsewhere.

Journalist Carmel Thomason's first book, the bestselling *Every Moment Counts: A life of Mary Butterwick*, was listed in the Top 10 Christian books by *Church Times*, Amazon and WHSmith. Carmel's latest book, *Against the Odds*, presents the true stories of eight people who have uncovered the strength and peace that freely offering forgiveness can bring in some of the most extreme situations.

If you enjoy reading about the Celtic church, Ray Simpson is a name you will recognise. In his latest book, *Hilda of Whitby*, Ray takes us to the seventh century AD to meet a highly influential, if little-known woman who became a significant figure in the development of the infant British church amid the chaos of the Anglo-Saxon years.

Also in the reviews that follow are a new devotional commentary on the Psalms, a resource for anyone looking for new preaching or group study ideas, and a book intriguingly entitled *Edible Bible Crafts*. This is just a taste (yes, pun intended!) of our summer publications for 2014.

To order, please complete the order form at the back of your Bible reading notes, visit www.brfonline.org.uk or ring our Customer Service team on 01865 319700.

You can also receive regular BRF book information, offers and ministry news direct into your inbox by signing up at www.brfonline.org.uk/enews-signup/

Against the Odds
True stories of healing and forgiveness
Carmel Thomason

'The old law of an eye for an eye leaves everybody blind' (Martin Luther King Jr.)

The act of forgiveness doesn't sit easily with our natural desire for justice. If something happens that is perceived as unfair, there is something deep inside that demands the wrong to be made right. It is a call we recognise in ourselves, hear in conversations and see as an essential part of most news stories that stream from newspapers, radio and TV daily. Against this inner demand stands the instruction of Jesus to forgive not once but continually. How can we reconcile these two apparent extremes?

Carmel Thomason presents the testimonies of eight people who have more reason than most not to forgive and yet, in the darkest of situations, have discovered the release and peace that forgiveness brings.

The book is split into two parts. The testimonies in Part 1 come from stories of war, crime and terrorism, events that most of us will not have to experience. They remind us all, however, that behind the breaking news story are real people, deeply hurt by events from which they need to find a way to rebuild and move on.

In Part 2, Carmel presents testimonies of everyday stories of forgiveness, which challenge us to ask, 'Are we keeping a record of rights and wrongs against those we love or have loved, or against ourselves, which is harming us not only as human beings but also as Christians?'

In both parts of the book, after each testimony is a short reflection on the story, drawing out its implications for understanding forgiveness. Questions are also provided for reading groups.

pb, 978 1 84101 739 6, £8.99

The Psalms
A commentary for reflection and prayer
Henry Wansbrough

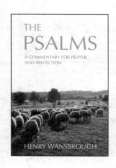

A compilation of the daily readings on the Psalms written by one of the UK's leading Catholic scholars, Henry Wansbrough OSB, for BRF's *Guidelines* Bible reading notes. The commentary, which covers all 150 psalms, draws on current biblical scholarship, providing insight into the background (historical, literary and cultural) of each psalm and illustrated from Henry's own years of living and working in the Middle East. The commentary is a helpful companion for personal devotion as well as for preaching.

pb, 978 1 84101 648 1, £8.99

Hilda of Whitby
A spirituality for now
Ray Simpson

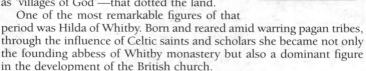

In the dark and turbulent centuries after the Roman occupation, which witnessed the invasion and colonisation of vast areas of the country by Anglo-Saxon tribes, the gospel light continued to shine across Britain through the witness of the monastic communities—known as 'villages of God'—that dotted the land.

One of the most remarkable figures of that period was Hilda of Whitby. Born and reared amid warring pagan tribes, through the influence of Celtic saints and scholars she became not only the founding abbess of Whitby monastery but also a dominant figure in the development of the British church.

Ray Simpson, international speaker, author and founding Guardian of the Community of Aidan and Hilda, investigates the drama of Hilda's life and ministry and presents the spiritual lessons we can draw for Christian life and leadership today. Published to coincide with the 1400th anniversary of Hilda's birth.

pb, 978 1 84101 728 0, £7.99

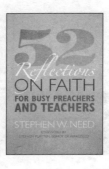

52 Reflections on Faith for Busy Preachers and Teachers
From the Sinai summits to the Emmaus road
Stephen W. Need

Formerly a New Testament Studies tutor and now a priest in Chelmsford Diocese, Stephen W. Need offers a wealth of personal inspiration for preachers as well as stimulating material for group study in these 52 reflections on selected stories from the Bible. He explores both biblical and theological dimensions and also makes connections with wider culture.

The book is split into two main sections: the first part provides reflections for the Sundays of the Christian year, from Advent to the feast of Christ the King, while the second part offers reflections that consider core aspects of Christian belief.

pb, 978 1 84101 743 3, £9.99

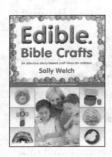

Edible Bible Crafts
64 delicious story-based craft ideas for children
Sally Welch

A range of edible crafts for 3- to 11-year-olds, covering twelve Old Testament and twelve New Testament stories and eight key festivals from the church year. Each unit gives the Bible story in a children's version, a short reflection on the passage, and both sweet and savoury recipe ideas. The recipes use readily available ingredients and equipment, require no cooking during the craft session and can be used in a variety of situations, including Sunday schools, midweek clubs and Messy Church events.

The book includes detailed information about set-up and preparation, tips on where to buy ingredients, and recipes to form the basis of the crafts.

pb, 978 0 85746 243 5, £11.99

To order copies of any of these books, please turn to the order form on page 155, or visit www.brfonline.org.uk.

As a Christian charity, BRF is involved in seven distinct yet complementary areas.

- **BRF** (www.brf.org.uk) resources adults for their spiritual journey through Bible reading notes, books and Quiet Days. BRF also provides the infrastructure that supports our other specialist ministries.
- **Foundations21** (www.foundations21.net) provides flexible and innovative ways for individuals and groups to explore their Christian faith and discipleship through a multimedia internet-based resource.
- **Messy Church** (www.messychurch.org.uk), led by Lucy Moore, enables churches all over the UK (and increasingly abroad) to reach children and adults beyond the fringes of the church.
- **Barnabas in Churches** (www.barnabasinchurches.org.uk) helps churches to support, resource and develop their children's ministry with the under-11s more effectively.
- **Barnabas in Schools** (www.barnabasinschools.org.uk) enables primary school children and teachers to explore Christianity creatively and bring the Bible alive within RE and Collective Worship.
- **Faith in Homes** (www.faithinhomes.org.uk) supports families to explore and live out the Christian faith at home.
- **Who Let The Dads Out** (www.wholetthedadsout.org) inspires churches to engage with dads and their pre-school children.

At the heart of BRF's ministry is a desire to equip adults and children for Christian living—helping them to read and understand the Bible, explore prayer and grow as disciples of Jesus. We need your help to make an impact on the local church, local schools and the wider community.

- You could support BRF's ministry with a one-off gift or regular donation (using the response form on page 153).
- You could consider making a bequest to BRF in your will.
- You could encourage your church to support BRF as part of your church's giving to home mission—perhaps focusing on a specific area of our ministry, or a particular member of our Barnabas team.
- Most important of all, you could support BRF with your prayers.

If you would like to discuss how a specific gift or bequest could be used in the development of our ministry, please phone 01865 319700 or email enquiries@brf.org.uk.

Whatever you can do or give, we thank you for your support.

BIBLE READING RESOURCES PACK

Thank you for reading BRF Bible reading notes. BRF has been producing a variety of Bible reading notes for over 90 years, helping people all over the UK and the world connect with the Bible on a personal level every day.

Could you help us find other people who would enjoy our notes?

We produce a Bible Reading Resource Pack for church groups to use to encourage regular Bible reading.

This FREE pack contains:

- Samples of all BRF Bible reading notes.
- Our Resources for Personal Bible Reading catalogue, providing all you need to know about our Bible reading notes.
- A ready-to-use church magazine feature about BRF notes.
- Ready-made sermon and all-age service ideas to help your church into the Bible (ideal for Bible Sunday events).
- And much more!

How to order your FREE pack:

- Visit: www.biblereadingnotes.org.uk/request-a-bible-reading-resources-pack/
- Telephone: 01865 319700 between 9.15 and 17.30
- Post: Complete the form below and post to: Bible Reading Resource Pack, BRF, 15 The Chambers, Vineyard, Abingdon, OX14 3FE

Name _____

Address _____

_____

_____ Postcode _____

Telephone _____

Email _____

Please send me _____ Bible Reading Resources Pack(s)

This pack is produced free of charge for all UK addresses but, if you wish to offer a donation towards our costs, this would be appreciated. If you require a pack to be sent outside of the UK, please contact us for details of postage and packing charges. Tel: +44 1865 319700. Thank you.

BRF MINISTRY APPEAL RESPONSE FORM

I want to help BRF by funding some of its core ministries. Please use my gift for:
❏ Where most needed ❏ Barnabas Children's Ministry ❏ Foundations21
❏ Messy Church ❏ Who Let The Dads Out?

Please complete all relevant sections of this form and print clearly.

Title _____ First name/initials _____ Surname _____
Address _____
_____ Postcode _____
Telephone _____ Email _____

Regular giving

If you would like to give by standing order, please contact Debra McKnight (tel: 01235 462305; email debra.mcknight@brf.org.uk; write to BRF address).

If you would like to give by direct debit, please tick the box below and fill in details:

❏ I would like to make a regular gift of £ _____ per month / quarter / year
(delete as appropriate) by Direct Debit. (Please complete the form on page 159.)

One-off donation

Please accept my special gift of
❏ £10 ❏ £50 ❏ £100 (other) £ _____ by

❏ Cheque / Charity Voucher payable to 'BRF'
❏ Visa / Mastercard / Charity Card
(delete as appropriate)

Name on card _____

Card no. ☐☐☐☐ ☐☐☐☐ ☐☐☐☐ ☐☐☐☐

Start date ☐☐☐☐   Expiry date ☐☐☐☐

Security code ☐☐☐

Signature _____ Date _____

❏ I would like to give a legacy to BRF. Please send me further information.

If you would like to Gift Aid your donation, please fill in the form overleaf.

Please detach and send this completed form to: Debra McKnight, BRF,
15 The Chambers, Vineyard, Abingdon OX14 3FE. BRF is a Registered Charity (No.233280)

GIFT AID DECLARATION

Bible Reading Fellowship

Please treat as Gift Aid donations all qualifying gifts of money made
today ☐   in the past 4 years ☐   in the future ☐   (tick all that apply)

I confirm I have paid or will pay an amount of Income Tax and/or Capital Gains Tax for each tax year (6 April to 5 April) that is at least equal to the amount of tax that all the charities that I donate to will reclaim on my gifts for that tax year. I understand that other taxes such as VAT or Council Tax do not qualify. I understand the charity will reclaim 25p of tax on every £1 that I give on or after 6 April 2008.

Donor's details

Title _____ First name or initials _____ Surname _____

Full home address _____

_____

Postcode _____

Date _____

Signature _____

Please notify Bible Reading Fellowship if you:
* want to cancel this declaration
* change your name or home address
* no longer pay sufficient tax on your income and/or capital gains.

If you pay Income Tax at the higher or additional rate and want to receive the additional tax relief due to you, you must include all your Gift Aid donations on your Self-Assessment tax return or ask HM Revenue and Customs to adjust your tax code.

BRF PUBLICATIONS ORDER FORM

Please send me the following book(s):

		Quantity	Price	Total
688 7	Creative Prayer Ideas (C. Daniel)	_____	£8.99	_____
728 0	Hilda of Whitby (R. Simpson)	_____	£7.99	_____
584 2	Transformed by the Beloved (D. Munoz)	_____	£6.99	_____
739 6	Against the Odds (C. Thomason)	_____	£8.99	_____
648 1	The Psalms (H. Wansbrough)	_____	£8.99	_____
743 3	52 Reflections for Busy Preachers (S.W. Need)	_____	£9.99	_____
146 9	A Good Childhood (L. Baddaley)	_____	£6.99	_____
163 6	Parenting Children for a Life of Purpose (R. Turner)	_____	£8.99	_____
243 5	Edible Bible Crafts (S. Welch)	_____	£11.99	_____

Total cost of books £ _____
Donation £ _____
Postage and packing £ _____
TOTAL £ _____

POSTAGE AND PACKING CHARGES				
order value	UK	Europe	Surface	Air Mail
£7.00 & under	£1.25	£3.00	£3.50	£5.50
£7.01–£30.00	£2.25	£5.50	£6.50	£10.00
Over £30.00	free	prices on request		

Please complete the payment details below and send with payment to: **BRF, 15 The Chambers, Vineyard, Abingdon OX14 3FE**

Name _____

Address _____

_____ Postcode

Tel _____ Email _____

Total enclosed £ _____ (cheques should be made payable to 'BRF')

Please charge my Visa ❑ Mastercard ❑ Switch card ❑ with £

Card no: ☐☐☐☐ ☐☐☐☐ ☐☐☐☐ ☐☐☐☐ ☐☐☐☐

Expires ☐☐☐☐ Security code ☐☐☐

Issue no (Switch only) ☐☐☐☐

Signature (essential if paying by credit/Switch) _____

GUIDELINES INDIVIDUAL SUBSCRIPTIONS

❏ I would like to take out a subscription myself:

Your name _____

Your address _____

_____ Postcode _____

Tel _____ Email _____

Please send *Guidelines* beginning with the September 2014 / January 2015 / May 2015 issue: (delete as applicable)

(please tick box)	UK	SURFACE	AIR MAIL
GUIDELINES	❏ £15.99	❏ £23.25	❏ £25.50
GUIDELINES 3-year sub	❏ £40.50		
GUIDELINES PDF download	❏ £12.75 (UK and overseas)		

Please complete the payment details below and send with appropriate payment to: **BRF, 15 The Chambers, Vineyard, Abingdon OX14 3FE**

Total enclosed £ _____ (cheques should be made payable to 'BRF')

Please charge my Visa ❏ Mastercard ❏ Switch card ❏ with £ _____

Card no: ⬚⬚⬚⬚⬚⬚⬚⬚⬚⬚⬚⬚⬚⬚⬚⬚⬚⬚

Expires ⬚⬚⬚⬚ Security code ⬚⬚⬚

Issue no (Switch only) ⬚⬚⬚⬚

Signature (essential if paying by card) _____

To set up a direct debit, please also complete the form on page 159 and send it to BRF with this form.

BRF is a Registered Charity

GL0214

GUIDELINES GIFT SUBSCRIPTIONS

❑ I would like to give a gift subscription (please provide both names and addresses:

Your name _____

Your address _____

_____ Postcode _____

Tel _____ Email _____

Gift subscription name _____

Gift subscription address _____

_____ Postcode _____

Gift message (20 words max. or include your own gift card for the recipient)

_____

_____

Please send *Guidelines* beginning with the September 2014 / January 2015 / May 2015 issue: (delete as applicable)

(please tick box)	UK	SURFACE	AIR MAIL
GUIDELINES	❑ £15.99	❑ £23.25	❑ £25.50
GUIDELINES 3-year sub	❑ £40.50		
GUIDELINES PDF download	❑ £12.75 (UK and overseas)		

Please complete the payment details below and send with appropriate payment to: **BRF, 15 The Chambers, Vineyard, Abingdon OX14 3FE**

Total enclosed £ _____ (cheques should be made payable to 'BRF')

Please charge my Visa ❑ Mastercard ❑ Switch card ❑ with £ _____

Card no: ☐☐☐☐ ☐☐☐☐ ☐☐☐☐ ☐☐☐☐ ☐☐☐☐ ☐☐☐☐

Expires ☐☐☐☐ Security code ☐☐☐

Issue no (Switch only) ☐☐☐☐

Signature (essential if paying by card) _____

To set up a direct debit, please also complete the form on page 159 and send it to BRF with this form.

DIRECT DEBIT PAYMENTS

Now you can pay for your annual subscription to BRF notes using Direct Debit. You need only give your bank details once, and the payment is made automatically every year until you cancel it. If you would like to pay by Direct Debit, please use the form opposite, entering your BRF account number under 'Reference'.

You are fully covered by the Direct Debit Guarantee:

The Direct Debit Guarantee

- This Guarantee is offered by all banks and building societies that accept instructions to pay Direct Debits.
- If there are any changes to the amount, date or frequency of your Direct Debit, The Bible Reading Fellowship will notify you 10 working days in advance of your account being debited or as otherwise agreed. If you request The Bible Reading Fellowship to collect a payment, confirmation of the amount and date will be given to you at the time of the request.
- If an error is made in the payment of your Direct Debit, by The Bible Reading Fellowship or your bank or building society, you are entitled to a full and immediate refund of the amount paid from your bank or building society.
  - – If you receive a refund you are not entitled to, you must pay it back when The Bible Reading Fellowship asks you to.
- You can cancel a Direct Debit at any time by simply contacting your bank or building society. Written confirmation may be required. Please also notify us.

The Bible Reading Fellowship

Instruction to your bank or building society to pay by Direct Debit

Please fill in the whole form using a ballpoint pen and send to The Bible Reading Fellowship, 15 The Chambers, Vineyard, Abingdon OX14 3FE.

Service User Number: | 5 | 5 | 8 | 2 | 2 | 9 |

Name and full postal address of your bank or building society

To: The Manager	Bank/Building Society
Address	
	Postcode

Name(s) of account holder(s)

Branch sort code

Bank/Building Society account number

Reference

Instruction to your Bank/Building Society

Please pay The Bible Reading Fellowship Direct Debits from the account detailed in this instruction, subject to the safeguards assured by the Direct Debit Guarantee.
I understand that this instruction may remain with The Bible Reading Fellowship and, if so, details will be passed electronically to my bank/building society.

Signature(s)
Date

Banks and Building Societies may not accept Direct Debit instructions for some types of account.

This page is intentionally left blank.